House Beautiful
COLORS FOR YOUR HOME

493 DESIGNER FAVORITES

EXPANDED
EDITION

House Beautiful
COLORS FOR YOUR HOME
493 DESIGNER FAVORITES

EXPANDED
EDITION

HEARST BOOKS

New York

HEARST BOOKS

New York

An Imprint of Sterling Publishing
387 Park Avenue South
New York, NY 10016

ISBN 978-1-61837-133-1

Distributed in Canada by Sterling Publishing
c/o Canadian Manda Group, 165 Dufferin Street
Toronto, Ontario, Canada M6K 3H6

Distributed in the United Kingdom by GMC Distribution Services
Castle Place, 166 High Street, Lewes, East Sussex, England BN7 1XU

Distributed in Australia by Capricorn Link (Australia) Pty. Ltd.
P.O. Box 704, Windsor, NSW 2756, Australia

For information about custom editions, special sales, and premium and
corporate purchases, please contact Sterling Special Sales at 800-805-5489
or specialsales@sterlingpublishing.com.

Manufactured in China

2 4 6 8 10 9 7 5 3 1

www.sterlingpublishing.com

MORNING GLORY

UTAH SKY

DARK ROYAL BLUE

WINDMILL WINGS

PALE MOON

COOKING APPLE GREEN

SPRING IRIS

AUTUMN CROCUS

COLONIAL ROSE

🖌 CONTENTS 🖌

FOWLER PINK

ORIENTAL IRIS

SUNDANCE

SASSY BLUE

PATRIOT BLUE

COLONY GREEN

RIVIERA AZURE

PERIDOT

CORAL GABLES

What's your favorite color?

INTRODUCTION

What's your favorite color?

You've been asked that question hundreds of times, and answered without skipping a beat. It is a very simple question—until it's time to choose a paint color for the walls of your home. Then, all of a sudden, it's surprisingly hard. Who hasn't struggled to pick a cream that wasn't too yellow or a blue that wasn't too cold?

No more struggling. The colors you're looking for are in this book. Based on *House Beautiful*'s most popular column, this little volume is filled with more than 493 paint formulas that professional interior designers have used successfully in their own rooms. It explains why they work and where they work best. These are the colors you've been trying to find— colors you can live with happily for years.

House Beautiful offers its deepest appreciation to all the designers who have shared their hard-earned expertise in color and décor. Their paint selections and commentary provide rare insight into what makes color work. Thanks to their extraordinary generosity, you, too, can make their favorite colors your own.

CHAPTER 1

THE BASICS

TAKING
THE PLUNGE

Timidity can keep you trapped in bland surroundings. Let these fearless designers ease you down a more colorful path. Follow their lead and you'll never turn back.

In a Connecticut lake cottage, designer Gil Schafer and color consultant Eve Ashcraft chose Narragansett Green for the porch's trim and floor, and Stonington Gray for the ceiling, creating a natural transition between indoors and out.

GIL SCHAFER AND EVE ASHCRAFT
BENJAMIN MOORE | NARRAGANSETT GREEN HC-157
| STONINGTON GRAY HC-170

PETER DUNHAM

RALPH LAUREN PAINT | OYSTER BAY SS61

"Take this incredible turquoisey blue-green, like you'd see on a cloisonné vase, and paint it on the reverse side of glass. Then use it as a tabletop. You have the effect of color, once removed — even the most color-phobic will usually go for it. And it looks so glossy and deep. Absolutely ravishing."

ELISSA CULLMAN

BENJAMIN MOORE | SILKEN PINE 2144-50

"Pale green is a kind of universal donor. Even our most beige clients seem to respond well to green, probably because it's a color we see so much in nature. This is a soft, celadony green, like a piece of the palest jade. I'll often use it in a master bedroom."

ANTONIO DA MOTTA

DONALD KAUFMAN COLOR COLLECTION | DKC-17

"A hallway tends to be a dead space, but paint it this warm Etruscan red and it's a blast of life. You don't have to live in it. You're just walking through. But it's a hook. People can get addicted to color after they paint a hallway."

Wainscoting and woodwork painted in a light white set off the blue-gray walls of this entry hall and stairway wall, designed by Madeline Stuart.

MADELINE STUART
FARROW & BALL | LIGHT BLUE 22

"I'm always surprised when clients balk at color and never surprised when they realize the difference it makes. In a transitional space like a stair hall, you have more freedom, so we tried a grayish modified blue—soft, but with great depth. Once the client saw how it enriched the space, the deal was done."

"After we bought the place we were flying up from Florida to Atlanta, and as we came through the clouds I said, 'This is what I want to wake up to every morning, a feeling of lightness and airiness, like we're floating on a meringue.' Polished woods and shots of gold—the gilt of a picture frame, the dull brass of a chandelier—warm the palette up and bring it to life."

PHOEBE HOWARD FARROW & BALL | CLUNCH 2009

CHERYL KATZ

BENJAMIN MOORE | COASTAL FOG AC-1

"This is a color for people who think they want all white. It's a warm gray with a little hint of green—a good choice for a living room since it still lets you have a neutral envelope, but it's not boring. Cool it down with icy blues, or warm it up with mustard."

SCOTT SANDERS

BENJAMIN MOORE | CORAL REEF 012

"Don't give guests a white room—they probably have that at home. Take a chance on this bright coral, softer than orange and more hip than pink. Very Palm Beach and lobster salad on a summer day."

BARRY DIXON
FARROW & BALL
| PICTURE GALLERY RED 42 (LEFT)
| FOWLER PINK 39 (RIGHT)
"I took the color of a seashell—actually, it was the inside lip of a conch where it goes into this rosy, fleshy tone—and then re-created it with three parts Picture Gallery Red to one part Fowler Pink. If you can find the color somewhere in nature, it often makes people feel more comfortable."

KATHRYN M. IRELAND

FARROW & BALL | BORROWED LIGHT 235

"Start with something pale. Then add more color, if you like, with fabric. This is a beautiful, restful blue, very soft on the eye. Lends itself particularly well to antiques and faded fabrics."

KEITH IRVINE

BENJAMIN MOORE | UTAH SKY 2065-40

"It's a clean, simple jolt of blue. Simple, like all good American traditions, and I would use it in an entrance hall, against a clear white trim. The next injection of color will be a hell of a lot easier."

SUZANNE LOVELL

DONALD KAUFMAN COLOR COLLECTION | DKC-66

"I'd go straight to the library and paint it this deep, luscious purplish brown, like the bark of a tree when it's wet in the rain. A dark color actually expands the space, because it erases the boundaries. Then the room becomes all about the books and the art."

TODD KLEIN

BENJAMIN MOORE | MAN ON THE MOON OC-106

"The client wanted yellow in the living room but was afraid to commit, so we landed on this wonderful warm cream, the color of a magnolia petal. As the day wanes, it gets deeper and really starts to glow once the lights are turned on. Who doesn't need a little moonglow in their life?"

NOEL JEFFREY

BENJAMIN MOORE | MORNING GLORY 785

"Do this soft blue in a bedroom, and it would be like waking up to a clear bright morning. If the person is really nervous about color, paint all the trim white. Do white furniture, white fabrics, white bed linens—then you can have a blue room without hitting them over the head with it."

The ceiling was glazed in a custom off-white
with a touch of gold to pick up on the glint of
all the acting awards.

TRIED AND TRUE CLASSICS

We called interior decorators with long, distinguished careers and asked: What "classic" palettes do you always come back to? Their answers may surprise you.

"I'm mad about this dark inky blue, as it gives great vibrancy and depth to a wall—especially if you put a topcoat of good clear varnish over it. That's what we did in Rex Harrison's Manhattan apartment in this fabulous little dining alcove. You can almost see yourself reflected in it."

KEITH IRVINE
BENJAMIN MOORE | DARK ROYAL BLUE 2065-20

ROSE TARLOW
FARROW & BALL | ALL WHITE 2005 (TOP)

| POINTING 2003 (CENTER)

| SLIPPER SATIN 2004 (BOTTOM)

"I never paint every wall in a room the same color. Light hits each wall in a different way, so I have to adjust the shade. It's usually white, but not one white. All White is a pure white, Pointing has a little ocher, and Slipper Satin has more gray. One of the most important things is how the shadows fall. That can be the most beautiful of all."

JOHN SALADINO
BENJAMIN MOORE | ORIENTAL IRIS 1418

"I'm emotionally attracted to periwinkle blue. It goes from gray into blue into lavender, depending on the time of day and month of year and the person looking at it. Blue combines two things I love, the ocean and the sky, which lifts me out of the quagmire of reality. It's a kind of bath. It represents a cleansing."

The walls in this master bedroom, designed by Phoebe Howard are painted in Farrow & Ball's Slipper Satin 2004.

DAVID EASTON

PAPERS & PAINTS LTD. | MOORISH RED HC55

"You can see the ground-up pigment in this paint, which gives it depth and a little iridescence. It's not flat, like American paints. It conjures up Greek vases and the walls of Knossos. It has the weight of antiquity."

BARBARA WESTBROOK

DONALD KAUFMAN COLOR COLLECTION | DKC-5

"It's a small bathroom, so I wanted everything built-in, precise, and neat. And yet it turned out charming and inviting. You wouldn't believe the number of people who pass through it and say they're dying to get into that bathtub."

BETTY SHERRILL

FARROW & BALL | MINSTER GREEN 224

"Green is my favorite color. It's just so soothing, and I think a library should be a soothing dark color. Wood, if you can have it. If you can't, make it this woodsy green. I like it glazed. I think any paint color is better glazed—it has more depth."

WILLIAM HODGINS

BENJAMIN MOORE | DECK ENAMEL RICH BROWN 60 (TOP)
| DECK ENAMEL BLACK C-112-80
(BOTTOM)

"It's a great formula—rich brown mixed half and half with black. It's just a beautiful dark brown with some gloss to it. Try it with white trim and a touch of pink."

CHARLOTTE MOSS

FARROW & BALL | VERT DE TERRE 234

"This is the furry, fuzzy green of lamb's ears. Very herbal. It's rich without being too saturated, and makes a great backdrop for mahogany, silver, or ivory. It's the color of my fantasy room—a book-lined great ballroom with a lit Polonaise in the middle of the limestone floor and orange trees in tubs. A pavilion in the forest."

VICENTE WOLF

BENJAMIN MOORE | PATRIOTIC WHITE 2135-70

"When the sun streams in, the walls read white, and then, as the day progresses, the color comes out. At night, the room is bathed in a pale, pale blue-green. I love the mercurial quality of it. It looks beautiful by the ocean, because it echoes the subtleties of the sea."

SALLY SIRKIN LEWIS

BENJAMIN MOORE | SMOKEY TAUPE 983

"This is the color of a beautiful Belgian linen. Very classic. Not too light and not too dark, but with enough depth to look great on a wall. Natural materials like limestone and granite look great against it. Bring in black lacquer, white upholstery, and red for an accent."

MARIO BUATTA

BENJAMIN MOORE | SUNDANCE 2022-50

"This is a medium-strength yellow, the color of fresh pineapple. People love it. It's just a happy color. Try it in a living room or dining room with a pale blue ceiling and white woodwork. It's like sunshine. Everything looks good against it—blue-and-white porcelain, a floral chintz."

FARROW & BALL | MATCHSTICK 2013
A pair of old rounded corbels from a church ceiling were
turned into wall anchors for these elegant canopy beds.
Two coats of a bright white high-gloss paint gave them a
dramatic effect against the warmly evocative Matchstick,
by **Farrow & Ball**.

Crisp white walls balance dark-wood furnishings in a room designed by Betsy Brown, who strives to create "a harmony of opposites."

WHICH WHITE IS THE BEST WHITE?

It's the ideal backdrop for fine art, an appropriate emphasis for architecture, and a noncompetitive companion for all other color. No wonder we love white: It brings the best qualities of every room to light.

"I love color, but I think it should either declare itself the major player in a composition or quietly add the crucial notes that balance a room and make it intriguing. I usually opt for the latter."

BETSY BROWN
PRATT & LAMBERT | SILVER LINING 32-32

OPPOSITE PAGE:

"It's the classic formula. Linen White looks as if it's been on the wall a long time, which works very well with old English and French furniture. But it can be a little too yellow, so I usually cool it down with Decorators White to make something a bit lighter and more sophisticated."

KEITH IRVINE

BENJAMIN MOORE | LINEN WHITE INTERIOR ROOM
MIXED WITH
| DECORATOR'S WHITE INT. RM.

PETER PENNOYER

FARROW & BALL | STRONG WHITE 2001

"If you have a wall with a bow in it or a floor that has settled, this will make an old room feel graceful rather than brand new. It has more pigment and therefore more character."

JEROME NEUNER

BENJAMIN MOORE | SUPER WHITE INTERIOR ROOM

"After testing every conceivable white and even mixing some ourselves, we wound up using this off-the-shelf paint in the galleries of the Museum of Modern Art. It's bright and clean, yet still has a little warmth to it."

ALEXA HAMPTON

BENJAMIN MOORE | IVORY WHITE 925

"This color looks great everywhere. It's a creamy, buttery white that my father (decorator Mark Hampton) liked to use, but I'm even more obsessive about it. Try an eggshell finish on the walls to reflect light but not look too glossy."

MARIETTE HIMES GOMEZ

DONALD KAUFMAN COLOR COLLECTION | DKC-51

"You can see every color in it—it's a chameleon that changes with natural light. Anything you put near it is comfortable. This white is going to be with me for the rest of my life."

. . . .

MURRAY MOSS

BENJAMIN MOORE | SUPER WHITE INTERIOR ROOM

"Everything looks good against a true, clear, eye-chilling, freezing-cold white. It's like a blizzard, or Ascot, or Huck Finn's white fence, or marsh-mallows, or sugar. Anything placed against that background projects like Technicolor."

. . . .

THOMAS JAYNE

BENJAMIN MOORE | ACADIA WHITE OC-38

"It has a nice green cast to it; perfect for a summer house in a leafy setting. It acts as a bridge to the outdoors."

CRAIG SCHUMACHER AND PHILIP KIRK
BEHR PAINTS | PLANTATION WHITE WN-18
Craig Schumacher and Phillip Kirk painted the bead-
board walls and ceiling of this bedroom a warm white,
creating an effective "gallery" for a collection of paintings, drawings, prints, and photographs. The white
gives the walls a lovely rustic sort of whitewash feel.

JUSTINE CUSHING
BENJAMIN MOORE | DECORATOR'S WHITE
INTERIOR ROOM

Justine Cushing designed this cozy country cottage in her
trademark chintz. She had the living room walls painted
Decorator's White by Benjamin Moore because of the
low ceilings.

RICHARD GLUCKMAN

BENJAMIN MOORE | CHINA WHITE INTERIOR ROOM

"You don't want a highly reflective wall surface if you're going to be hanging a lot of art. China White is a very subtle off-white with a gray tone that helps the work stand out."

JONATHAN ADLER

RALPH LAUREN PAINT | POCKET WATCH WHITE WW11

"When it comes to whites I use only Pocket Watch White. It's soft and warm but not cream, and still undeniably white. It will make a room look gracious and young at the same time."

KELLY WEARSTLER

PRATT & LAMBERT | SEED PEARL 27-32

"I put it on every ceiling in my house. It's a clean, crisp white that has a little bit of warmth in it, which gives it more depth and dimension. I use it on moldings for contrast."

THOMAS PHEASANT

BENJAMIN MOORE | IVORY WHITE 925

"It's tough to get a crisp look without being cold. Ivory White does the trick. It's the most flex-ible white I've come across and works with any color. Carry it from room to room on the trim."

In a sleek Manhattan apartment, the living room walls are bathed in **Bella Donna**, a smoky lavender neutral with both refinement and sex appeal.

SOOTHING
NEUTRALS

Neutrals are the starting point for almost any palette. But which neutrals? You can't go wrong making a commitment to a color that you love. Colors with a little zing go with everything.

"I've been using Bella Donna a lot. It's a smoky lavender gray, the color of a twilight sky. I used it on the parlor floor of a brownstone, and it looked flat-out sophisticated. I'm in the bedroom of my country house right now, which is painted this color. Bella Donna is a sexy, adult color, but it can go a lot of different ways."

DD ALLEN C2, BELLA DONNA | C2-316 W

CHRISTOPHER MAYA
BENJAMIN MOORE | GLASS SLIPPER 1632

"I love grayish blue as a backdrop—the blue of a washed-out sky just after a storm has passed. My office has this color on the walls. I have Swedish grayish-blue chairs, mahogany desk, a shiny modern chrome lamp, a painting done in black oils, and bright red curtains! Almost anything looks great with this blue. That's what neutrals are all about, aren't they?"

MATTHEW WHITE
BENJAMIN MOORE | SPRING MEADOW 486

"I like this soft, muted green. It's optimistic without being blatantly cheerful. It's light but also deep—a sophisticated green. Then at night, it turns darker and becomes more cocoon-like."

MATTHEW PATRICK SMYTH
BENJAMIN MOORE | LINEN WHITE 70

"When in doubt, Linen White: You can phone that in. It might seem like a cop-out, but it works beautifully. I use it when people are unsure. They want something light and airy but not stark white. No matter what light you put it in, it looks good."

KEN FULK

PHILIP'S PERFECT COLOR

| AGUA VERTE PPC-BL7 (LEFT)

| MINK PPC-G13 (RIGHT)

"The walls are a taupey brown. They're pretty rich. The Mink gives oomph and weight to live up to the architecture of the room, and the pale blue, which I've also used in the backs of the bookcases, makes it a little more playful and vaporous."

MICHAEL SMITH

PRATT & LAMBERT | SILVER BLOND 14-29

Michael Smith painted the cabinets and trim a soft butter-milk. Flooded with natural sunlight, the hue gives the kitchen a vintage feel. It also allows the colorful furnishings— the antique Chinese lanterns, the blue-washed table and chair, the warm stone countertop—to really pop.

CHRISTOPHER RIDOLFI

BENJAMIN MOORE | GRANT BEIGE HC-83

"My standby is Grant Beige. It's like a favorite pair of worn khakis. It fares equally well with the light of Texas or the East Coast."

MARY MCDONALD

DUNN-EDWARDS | COCONUT SKIN DE1055

"I could paint every room in the house Coconut Skin, a deep mocha brown with some milk in it. It's cozy and comforting without being kidsy: grounding with pastels, weighty with bright colors."

MARIETTE HIMES GOMEZ

FARROW & BALL | STRING 8 (TOP)
         | GREEN GROUND 206 (BOTTOM)

"Khaki and celadon are my picks. These are colors, but they're still very neutral in their integrity. Each one is softly beautiful. They don't scream. They don't dictate—you can put them with anything."

STEVEN GAMBREL

BENJAMIN MOORE | HORIZON 1478

"I always come back to Horizon, a pale gray that doesn't turn blue or green on you. It's a sophisticated background to so many interiors. Blues look beautiful against this gray, but so do pinks and lavenders."

GERRIE BREMERMANN

BENJAMIN MOORE | PAPAYA 957

"The most enduring color I've found looks like homemade vanilla ice cream with a little caramel in it. I love it with the blues, greens, and blue-greens of the sea and sky, and with various soft warm pinks. There's nothing edgy about it, which suits me fine."

OPPOSITE PAGE:

Kathy Smith used autumn colors—
brown, beige, and gold neutrals with a
splash of coral—to give this living room
depth and warmth. When you walk in,
you feel instantly enveloped and safe.

KATHY SMITH FARROW & BALL | BISCUIT 38

ELLEN KENNON

FULL SPECTRUM PAINTS | MUSHROOM

"Mushroom changes drastically—one minute putty
and the next, rosier. Chameleon-like and mysterious,
it takes on the properties of the colors around it."

JEFFREY BILHUBER

BENJAMIN MOORE | PALE VISTA 2029-60

"I use spring green as a neutral. It's the color of buds
and bulbs popping out of the ground after a long
winter—a reassuring color, great in a bedroom."

MALLORY MARSHALL

BENJAMIN MOORE | WENGE AF-180

"Wenge is the color of bitter chocolate with 70%
cacao that everyone's calling health food. A neutral
should get along with every color in the fan deck,
and this one is like the nicest girl in the sixth grade."

SUSAN FERRIER
BENJAMIN MOORE
DANVILLE TAN HC-91
"I think it's very important to limit color, to be restrained. I look for colors with good vibrations to create harmony with the eye. Here I used blue-grays, green-blues, and brown-greens. Every single color is hard to put your finger on."

JEFFREY BILHUBER

BENJAMIN MOORE | PEACE AND HAPPINESS 1380

"Lavender is the new beige. From lilac to amethyst, it's an extraordinary neutral and a great unifier—a soothing, peaceful color that is timeless."

DARRYL CARTER

BENJAMIN MOORE | LOOKOUT POINT 1646

"It's one of those elusive non-colors that reminds me of the time between morning dew and sunrise—a perfect marriage between pale blue. Whatever room you put it in, it creates a calm, serene mood."

STEVEN GAMBREL

BENJAMIN MOORE | SEA STAR 2123-30

"I like very pale teal. It's a nice background for highly textured washed-out beige textiles, and together they make a kind of faded beach story, pulling together the greens of the earth, the grays of the sky, and the blue-greens of the water."

KEN FULK

PHILIP'S PERFECT COLORS | ADOBE 08

"I'll be stoned for saying terra-cotta—but I have one really excellent color. The beautiful thing about it is that it is earthen and Old Worldy, but it can work in a modern setting, and it looks great with really dark floors or pale, washed-out oak."

MARY MCDONALD

BENJAMIN MOORE | ROMANTIC PINK 2004-70

"Anywhere you're going to use white, consider pastel pink instead—for walls, ceilings, furniture, and lampshades. Then paint your floors pastel pink! You can't believe how many colors look great with it. What people don't realize is that you can also make it masculine by adding deep, rich saturated hues to your color scheme—chocolate brown, dark gray, navy, or eggplant."

GERRIE BREMERMANN
BENJAMIN MOORE | RACCOON HOLLOW 978

"We just got back from France, where I couldn't help noticing that everything is painted what I call Avignon taupe—that flaxy natural color that's a little on the gray side."

JENNIFER GARRIGUES
SHERWIN-WILLIAMS | HONIED WHITE 7106

"It looks like white with sunlight in it. You can use it with saturated colors or the airiest whites and creams, and it works no matter what the light is, it never turns funny colors."

JACK YOUNG
BENJAMIN MOORE | CORAL SPICE 2170-40

"In the intense light of Palm Beach, real colors make great neutrals, but colors that are quieted down. I like pale coral for a living room. It looks great with aqua, rattan, and bamboo."

NANCY BRAITHWAITE
BENJAMIN MOORE | VAN BUREN BROWN HC-70

"Chocolate brown settles a room and receives creams, reds, yellows, and blues beautifully. If you have insipid architecture, you should definitely consider it because walls fade away."

A vaulted ceiling, alcove windows, and an unusual yellow give this master bedroom a sense of airiness and drama.

MADELINE STUART
FARROW & BALL | PALE HOUND 71

"It's one of the most fabulously odd colors. It's a slightly bilious yellow, not the easiest color, but it has such depth and nuance. Juxtaposed against the James White trim, it's so crisp and unexpected. I adore this color."

SARA BENGUR

DONALD KAUFMAN COLOR COLLECTION | DKC-20

"Ocher feels like a neutral to me—a deep, earthy yellow that reminds me of southern Italy and Turkey. It looks good with other earthy colors, like terra-cotta or gray-blue, and it is really beautiful with lilac, lime green, and aubergine. People look at it and say, "Oh no, I couldn't possibly." But the earthier colors can be really relaxing."

RICHARD GLUCKMAN

BENJAMIN MOORE | BEAR CREEK 1470

"This mysterious, warm sort of aubergine is great for painting exposed steel structural elements. I got it directly from the painter Francesco Clemente's studio. All the doors, window frames, railings, and steel structure are painted Bear Creek, with a concrete floor and pale green cement board walls—very beautiful."

VICENTE WOLF

BENJAMIN MOORE | GRAYTINT 1611

"I love pearl gray for a foyer, bedroom, or hallway—anywhere you want a sense of intimacy. If there's a big white space with a niche, I would paint only the niche this soft gray. I always like shadowy, mercurial colors that play up the mysteries of architecture."

PHOEBE HOWARD
FARROW & BALL
SHADED WHITE 201
Phoebe Howard painted her dining room walls a dark off-white, both unobtrusive and mellow, but kept it bright enough to make the best use of the natural light available.

BARBARA BARRY

DONALD KAUFMAN COLOR COLLECTION | DKC-8

"Green is the great neutral, all the way from pond scum to soft sage or pale celery. I recently moved into a new house surrounded by greenery, and when I was thinking of what color I might use for a drapery lining, it came to me to reflect the green that is present year-round right outside that window."

MALLORY MARSHALL

SHERWIN-WILLIAMS | DETERMINED ORANGE 6635

"Orange is a wonderful neutral. It can't be a washed-out orange—it has to be a color you'd want to lick, which is why the good oranges are always called Salsa or Punch."

KELLY WEARSTLER

PRATT & LAMBERT | DELFT BLUE 24-21

"This has some gray in it and a tiny bit of green. I'd use it in a family room, a den, even a bedroom. It's a little on the masculine side, but it still has some femininity. It just feels very rich and sensual."

DD ALLEN

C2 | SORCERER 5326

"I recently did a dining room with these dark blueberry walls, a chocolate brown rug, gold curtains, a mahogany table, and chairs upholstered in burgundy. Navy makes a great, sexy evening room—after all, it's the color of night."

CHRISTOPHER RIDOLFI

FARROW & BALL | COOKING APPLE GREEN 32

"It has gray in it, but there's still brightness within. To me it looks great with all metal finishes—bronze, wrought iron, nickel."

KATHY SMITH
SHERWIN-WILLIAMS | PALE EARTH 8133
Kathy Smith chose a subtle creamy beige for this master bathroom. It becomes vibrant when bathed in sunlight, exuding warmth and elegance with a very European kind of sophistication.

RUTHIE SOMMERS
BENJAMIN MOORE
ICEBERG 2122-50

"That unexpected bright blue is what made me fall in love with the house. It was such a great palette to start with. The natural inclination is to go pale—but the darker colors add punch. This is a house that screams, 'I'm at the beach! Relax!'"

SHARONE EINHORN AND HONEY WOLTERS
BENJAMIN MOORE | NOVEMBER RAIN 2142-60

"We just finished decorating a bungalow where we struggled picking paint colors because the owner had just stripped all the wood trim and didn't want to paint it. All the colors we picked changed totally in the presence of that orangey-light brown wood. A contractor finally told us about Benjamin Moore's November Rain—it's a putty color, warm but not too warm, and it looked great everywhere we put it."

MYRA HOEFER

FARROW & BALL | DOWN PIPE 26

"It's charcoal, but I think of it as wet stone, wet cement, or even soot. It's a fabulous color for trim—they use it in French and English houses all the time. In a kitchen, if you paint the walls and cabinets this color and use a lot of mirrors, you'd have a very rich, town housey, sexy alternative to the all-white kitchen."

ELLEN KENNON

FULL SPECTRUM PAINTS | BUTTERCREAM

"Buttercream is my favorite unexpected neutral. It's innately uplifting because it's the color of sunshine—an antidepressant with no side effects! But very pale yellow also soothes and looks great with rich, dark woods, blues, and greens. There's not a single color that doesn't work with it."

STEPHEN SILLS

BENJAMIN MOORE | STONE HARBOR 2111-50

"Any color can be a neutral if it is grayed off with a touch of black and used all over a room, without any other color interrupting it. I particularly love greens as neutrals: moss, sage, stone, hunter. I like to use many different tones."

FAYE CONE
DONALD KAUFMAN COLOR COLLECTION | DKC-54
Faye Cone chose a reflective neutral that echoes the rest of her bedroom. Here, pale ivory walls give the illusion of endless space without taking away from the natural beauty of the whitewashed bed frame.

AMELIA HANDEGAN

FINE PAINTS OF EUROPE | LP-16

"Butterscotch makes a nice burnished backdrop. It changes with the light—it can look like wheat or like a darker buff with an orange tone. At night it seems candlelit."

GARY MCBOURNIE

BENJAMIN MOORE | RED PARROT 1308

"Red has always been a neutral for me. I like it somewhere between claret and fire engine, so it's really red but with a slight bit of brown to it. It's cozy, glowing, and sexy."

TOM SCHEERER

PRATT & LAMBERT | DEEP JUNGLE 21-17

"I've always used what I call gardenia-leaf green. Put it on the walls and then bounce two other colors off it, like sky blue and coral pink. Fresh greens end up in virtually every room I put together."

MATTHEW PATRICK SMYTH

BENJAMIN MOORE | WICKHAM GRAY HC-171

"Lately I've been using a whole series of grays, everything from steel to a warm French gray. You want to be careful when picking your gray—nothing too sad, cold, or dingy."

VERSATILE BLUES

Elegant and ethereal. Deep and mysterious. Cool and icy. Bright and breezy. Cerulean blue, azure blue, robin's egg blue, indigo blue, sapphire blue. Every blue has a mood and personality. Every blue tells a story. Which blue tells yours?

The tiny guest room is the only room in David Jimenez's house given a deep wall color, a modern spin on the classic blue-and-white bedroom. It gives the space a distinctly masculine feel.

DAVID JIMENEZ
BENJAMIN MOORE | STARRY NIGHT BLUE 2067-20

RALPH HARVARD

SHERWIN-WILLIAMS/ DURON, COLORS OF HISTORIC
CHARLESTON | VERDITER BLUE, DCR078 NRH

"This is an intense 18th-century blue-green. They used to make it by pouring acids on copper and using the verdigris as the pigment for the paint."

WHITNEY STEWART

C2 | ELECTRIC 275

"What you want is an evening blue, an Yves Klein blue. It's contemplative, meditative, mysterious. When I want to be enveloped, blue is the only color that will do it for me."

WILLIAM DIAMOND AND ANTHONY BARATTA

SHERWIN-WILLIAMS | SASSY BLUE 1241

"Blue is my secret-agent color. I'm always sneaking it in these days. I guess it's like a bit of sky peeking out."

The turquoise on the walls looks even richer next to woodwork painted Benjamin Moore's Ivory White 925 (page 33) in the corner of this dining room by Markham Roberts.

MARKHAM ROBERTS
PARKER PAINT | WATERSIDE 7573M

"This bright, pretty turquoise reminds me of summers on Lake Michigan when I was a child, skipping stones and looking up at the sky, and feeling the sun on my body. Blue calms me and reenergizes me—just as the ocean does."

OPPOSITE PAGE :

The unexpected swimming pool blue in this entryway makes Ruthie Sommers' client fall in love with the whole house. It's a blue that evokes the spirit of the sea in this quintessential summer cottage.

RUTHIE SOMMERS

BENJAMIN MOORE | BLUE SEAFOAM 2056-60

HARRY HEISSMANN

VALSPAR | LYNDHURST CELESTIAL BLUE 5003-9C

"I like real colors, as opposed to those that are just a hint of something. I love clarity, and this is a clear blue. Anything you put against it—a black bamboo bed, a bright abstract painting—will pop."

THOMAS JAYNE

BENJAMIN MOORE | HEAVENLY BLUE 709

"This is the color of the sky in Old Master paintings, when the varnish has yellowed; it's luminous. Paint just the floor—you'd feel as if you were floating."

JAMIE DRAKE

BENJAMIN MOORE | WINDMILL WINGS 2067-60

"Blue is America's favorite color. It's certainly the most telegenic. That's why politicians wear blue shirts and why the White House pressroom is blue. It's cool. It's calming. This is an ethereal blue, with a touch of red that gives it a lavender cast."

DAVID KLEINBERG

BENJAMIN MOORE | COLONY GREEN 694

"I grew up in a house that was all turquoise, and for years I couldn't look at blue. But this color is so terrifically pretty and filled with joy—sort of like as if you were inside a robin's egg looking out into the light. I'd use it in a bedroom with white lacquered trim, a four-poster bed lacquered white, and crisp white bed linens."

ROBIN BELL

BENJAMIN MOORE | PADDINGTON BLUE 791

"This is a peacock blue, an exuberant blue that would set off all the objects in a room. I'd use it in a high-gloss finish with lots of white moldings. Blue is one of the best colors around for crispness and contrast. After all, what looks better than a naval officer in his dress blues?"

PHOEBE HOWARD
SHERWIN-WILLIAMS | BLUE HUBBARD 8438

"I just gravitate toward the softer blues and greens and sand colors. My client brought me a Jim Thompson silk ad that had all these bright blues and greens in it—cobalt, turquoise, lime, jade. She said, 'These colors. Take this with you.'"

MICHAEL OSTROW
BENJAMIN MOORE
DOLPHIN'S COVE 722
"This color is what we're known for. It's the Grace Home blue—a bright, crisp aqua that conjures up images of robin's eggs and gorgeous cerulean oceans. When we painted our store in L.A., every person would walk in, sigh, and say, 'I love this color—what is it?' It's soft enough to use in a bedroom and bold enough to hold its own in a dining room. You can push it in a lot of different directions."

T. KELLER DONOVAN
BENJAMIN MOORE | STUNNING 826

"The colors I like are very pure and uncomplicated. This is a nice, regular, all-American, patriotic, down-to-earth blue, with no weird tones in it. It's a happy blue. I used it in my kitchen, where it's a great background for all my antique Spode china—traditional, but still young, fun, and fresh."

ALEX PAPACHRISTIDIS
BENJAMIN MOORE | BLUE TOILE 748

"I like aqua blues. They're both calming and refreshing, and they always look so beautiful with brown wood floors and brown wood furniture. This particular shade has the glamour and dash of a Pucci dress and would be very stylish in an entry foyer, a powder room, or even a bedroom."

BARCLAY BUTERA
RALPH LAUREN PAINT | MYSTIC RIVER SS21

"This reminds me of one of those great English stately-homes sort of blues, because it's got a touch of gray in it. This is a very elegant color. I can see it in an entryway with a back-and-white marble floor and touches of pink and navy."

KENDALL WILKINSON
ANN HALL COLOR DESIGN | 39

"This is my signature, go-to blue. It's like a chameleon, changing from blue-gray to robin's egg to green-blue, depending on the light. It lets the room decide whether it's going to be neutral or bright. It's different in every setting. Once people try it, they tend to keep it forever."

TOM SCHEERER
FINE PAINTS OF EUROPE | DELFT BLUE 4003

"It's the easiest trick in the book—deep marine blue in high gloss with lots of white trim. You get something crisp and snappy without hardly trying and it instantly connotes that nautical feeling. And like any kind of dark room, it really shows off artwork."

CHARLOTTE MOSS
BENJAMIN MOORE | JAMESTOWN BLUE HC-148

"What Virginia girl wouldn't love Jamestown Blue? In certain lights, it's blue; in others, it has a haze of green. It's slate mixed with fog. And it's receptive to a range of partners, like Veronese gold, Chinese red, and cantaloupe. You can decorate with it. You can wear it."

SUSAN ZISES GREEN
BENJAMIN MOORE | RHYTHM AND BLUES 758

"This reminds me of a Tiffany box, and what's better than Tiffany? It's like a clear summer sky with a tinge of twilight on the horizon. I would use it on a porch with lots of wicker. Bring in pink, lime green. White, to keep it fresh. I used it in a kitchen and it really opened it up."

SHAZALYNN CAVIN-WINFREY
VALSPAR STILLNESS 7005-2

"I grew up in the desert in New Mexico and when I take my children home for a visit, we always say, 'Big blue sky!' Everywhere you look is this clear, pure blue, right down to the horizon line. It's the ultimate serenity for me. This paint color has the same kind of clarity. It gives this sitting rom the most natural, vibrant light."

JOHN GILMER
RALPH LAUREN PAINT | BALTIC BLUE IB86

"This is a true peacock blue, the blue of David Hockney's California swimming pools. It's a happy blue, beautiful and soothing during the day, but at night it comes alive, wrapping you in its warm, velvety embrace."

SUZANNE RHEINSTEIN
VALSPAR | EXOTIC SEA 5004-10B

"When I went to visit gardens in Normandy with the Garden Conservancy, I especially adored Brécy. Besides the surprise of a large Lalanne rabbit in the courtyard, the Versailles boxes are painted this marvelous blue, which I tried to duplicate. Go!"

DONALD KAUFMAN
DONALD KAUFMAN | DKC-96

"You know how you can have cloudy skies that look luminous? That's how this color feels. It's very atmospheric. It could fool you into thinking it's gray, but the blue comes out in dimmer light. People often object to the somber aspects of blue, but all you need to counteract that is white trim. When we see a high contrast of light and dark in a space, we think it's brighter than it is."

JEFFREY BILHUBER

BENJAMIN MOORE | VAN DEUSEN BLUE HC-156

"The Prussian blue gives this entrance hall a great sense of Arrival: It's triumphant," says Jeffrey. The regal shade is based on a color the designer had seen at Mount Vernon, George Washington's Virginia estate.

The walls and ceiling of this dining room are washed in a daring electric blue to bring drama to what was once a monotonous field of white. Glossy white trim breaks up the expanse, high-lighting the robust architectural details and adding dimension to the space.

TODD NICKEY
PRATT & LAMBERT | LAMBERT'S BLUE 25-13

ERIC COHLER
FARROW & BALL | CHINESE BLUE 90

"This is not too hot, not too cold, with a lot of green, which makes it feel grounded. Blue is so regenerative. There's the idea of water, renewal. It's powerful, regal—bluebloods, blue ribbons."

ELISSA CULLMAN
BENJAMIN MOORE | BLUE WAVE 2065-50

"Blue is tricky. It can go gray and sad. But not this warm Mediterranean blue. It's a bright, happy, not-a-cloud-in-the-sky blue, as if you're in vacation mode and having lobster and rosé at Tetou on the beach near Cannes."

In a Palm Beach entrance hall, designed by Lee
Beirly and Christopher Drake, saturated yellow
is set off by moldings painted with Benjamin
Moore White Dove semi-gloss enamel.

ENTERING THE HOME

It's the first space you see when you arrive home and the place where your guests form their first impression. If you want it to be inviting, color is the answer.

"It's one of those spaces that people go through quickly, so you can afford a higher level of drama. Often, there's no natural light, so you need a heavily saturated color like this warm, yolky yellow. Get it in full gloss because the gloss gives it depth, and it's much simpler to apply than glazing."

CHRISTOPHER DRAKE

BENJAMIN MOORE | SHOWTIME 923

ROBERT GOODWIN
BENJAMIN MOORE | IRON MOUNTAIN 2134-30
Robert Goodwin painted the trim the same dark blue-brown
as the walls to give it a modern spin. Everything in this
eclectic entryway is surprising: the rich taupe, the French
console, the English mirror, the Chinese porcelain, the
crazily gilt brackets.

KEITH IRVINE

BENJAMIN MOORE | SALSA 2009-20

"Red is the color of excitement, and I tend to go for corally orange reds. With red, you know you've arrived and you glance in the mirror and realize how great you look and breeze right in."

EVE ROBINSON

FARROW & BALL | DRAB 41

"I like a progression of color. It's good to start dark—this is so moody and has a wonderful earthy tone—and as you move inside, the rooms become lighter, which makes them seem more spacious."

JOHN OETGEN

BENJAMIN MOORE | PALLADIAN BLUE HC-144

"If you took green and sky blue and put them in a bucket with a lot of air, this is what you would get. I even put it on the ceiling. It looks great with black-and-white floors. I'd add a bronze bench with shocking pink upholstery."

PATRICIA HEALING

FINE PAINTS OF EUROPE | DUTCH CHOCOLATE 6012

"Imagine you're melting dark chocolate in a saucepan—that's the color. It glistens. This high-gloss paint looks almost like patent leather."

SUZANNE KASLER
BENJAMIN MOORE | ELEPHANT TUSK OC-8

With this project, the designer kept the whole house very tone on tone, with naturals, camels, tans, and browns. Here a clean ivory color allows the sculptural faux-bois balustrade and hand-colored engravings to really stand out.

T. KELLER DONOVAN
BENJAMIN MOORE | LINEN WHITE 70

"A hall takes such a beating. Mine looks like the shipping department at Macy's. So I'd choose a cool, calm white. Fill a mayonnaise jar with it and keep it in the closet for touch-ups."

JOHN BARMAN
RALPH LAUREN PAINT | RACER PINK 1B07

"It's a strong, vibrant pink, as masculine as you can get in a pink, with a nice shine to it. In a small entrance hall, I like to use deep strong colors to help define the space. Otherwise, you lose it."

STEVEN GAMBREL
PRATT & LAMBERT | ARGENT 1322

"Those 18th-century British architects kept the front hallway somber to recall the color of the stone outside, on the façade. I like the idea of bringing the outside in, but stone doesn't necessarily work for me. I tend to use a sky-bluish color that has a pretty heavy dose of gray and green."

An unexpected splash of bright lavender along the staircase wall sets a playful mood in the entry hall of this stone cottage designed by Eldon Wong.

ELDON WONG

BEHR'S DISNEY HOME CLASSIC POOH | BUTTERFLY FLUTTER BY DC2A-10-1

WHITNEY STEWART

C2 | QUAHOG 8385

"You want to make wow! but at the same time, you have to be neutral because it's the opener for the rest of the apartment. So what to do? Paint your hall this fabulous gray-taupe, which is still neutral but dark enough to make a statement."

WILLIAM R. EUBANKS

BENJAMIN MOORE | GOLDEN STRAW 2152-50

"I'm attracted to warm colors that kind of wrap their arms around you. This is like candlelight, with a wonderful golden glow. I'll put layers of glaze over it so it's as rich in daytime as it is at night."

T. KELLER DONOVAN
BENJAMIN MOORE | SUMMER SHOWER 2135-60
"A blue-and-white scheme brightens a room with no natural light. I chose Summer Shower because it has the coolness of the blue deep within a chunk of ice. Benjamin Moore's White Dove makes trim look tailored and crisp."

HERMES MALLEA

DONALD KAUFMAN COLOR COLLECTION | DKC-17

"We painted this tight little space an intense barn red. Everything around you was red—walls, ceilings, doors. You were completely encapsulated in red, so you couldn't really tell the dimensions."

KERRY JOYCE

SHERWIN-WILLIAMS | STUDIO MAUVE 0062

"This is a velvety gray with just the right amount of lavender. If it had any more lavender in it, it would be well beyond my pain threshold, but it doesn't, so it's perfect."

TOM BRITT

FINE PAINTS OF EUROPE | SPINNAKER WHITE 7032

"Right now, we're into this traditional oil paint in a color that looks like whipped cream. Get it in the Brilliant finish and it's very shiny, like gelato. Seriously, make your entry refreshing. Cool off."

RELAXING IN
THE LIVING ROOM

Looking to match your living room
to your personality? From passionate
reds to muted neutrals, bold blues to
sensual browns, get your inspiration
from the examples on these pages.

"Coral and sunflower yellow is a
palette I've used before. A mono-
chromatic beige scheme would
not have taken this house anywhere. I used a personal fabric
I developed. It's a fancy print by
Quadrille, but I had them run it for me on
orange and white mattress ticking to countrify it."

TOM SHEERER
BENJAMIN MOORE | MORNING SUNSHINE 2018-50

AMANDA KYSER
BENJAMIN MOORE | ONYX 2133-10
Here's a nice trick from designer Amanda Kyser: If you have a very large, open living room, you can divide the space up visually using a very dark contrasting color on the windows, baseboards and trim. This dark onyx helps to define the windows without making them gloomy.

JOE NYE
BENJAMIN MOORE | SHENANDOAH TAUPE AC-36
The cocoa brown color of this study is a dramatic depar-
ture from the rest of the house. Joe Nye wanted to give his
client one masculine, subdued room for a change of pace.
The room doubles as a guest bedroom and office, so the
quiet color is perfect.

JASON BELL

BENJAMIN MOORE
| SADDLE SOAP 2110-30
| TUDOR BROWN
| LADYBUG RED 1322

Jason Bell chose a dark olive for the walls, paired with a very rich brown on the trim and bookcases, for this non-traditional English country house. To add a hint of color, the back interiors of the bookshelves are painted a cheerful ladybug red, which nicely complements the red in the chair and sofa. It's cozy without being somber.

MYRA HOEFER

BENJAMIN MOORE | HORIZON GRAY 2141-50

"In this living room, there are many elegant things, lots of silks and textured velvets, but the wall color creates such a delicate, soft mood. I call it a non-color. It's like being inside a beautiful egg. You don't really know if it's a powder blue or a gray or a pale olive, but it's a color from nature, and it puts you at peace."

MARY McDONALD
BENJAMIN MOORE | LAVENDER ICE 2069-60
"I knew I wanted to bring green in here as an accent. But we wanted it more subtle and calming. I found a romantic, feminine, flowery Lee Jofa cotton print, which I put on a pair of slipper chairs I designed. The print has moss green washed-out chartreuse and a little bit of lavender gray in it. I pulled the lavender gray wall color from that."

RON WOODSON AND JAIME RUMMERFIELD
SHERWIN-WILLIAMS | LEAPFROG 6431

"You have to listen to what the house is asking for. For us, the blue and green combo is all about the beach. I think color can't be halfway or 'Hmmmm, should I?' It's all or nothing for us. There has to be a twist, something that's almost not natural to the combination."

This kitchen was set up primarily for entertaining,
with the big blond-wood center table as a buffet.

ENTERTAINING KITCHEN WALLS

When you're ready to break away from the classic white kitchen, where will you turn? Try these clean, fresh, and inviting alternatives.

The deep olive green color on the built-in millwork and cabinets was perfect. Chad Eisner chose this color to add depth and to show off the blond-wood center table.

CHAD EISNER

PRATT & LAMBERT | FLINT 32-20

CLARE DONOHUE
BENJAMIN MOORE | WEDGEWOOD GRAY HC-146 (TOP)
| WOODLAWN BLUE HC-147 (BOTTOM)

"Wedgewood Gray and Woodlawn Blue have that robin's egg vibe. I always hedge my bets toward grayed-down shades, because bright colors that look so happy in the paint store can look bizarre in real life. If you're nervous, start by painting the back wall inside the cabinets."

PAULA PERLINI

BENJAMIN MOORE | WARM SIENNA 1203

"Might as well make it cozy. Everybody comes in anyway—you can't beat them out with a spoon. Plates would look great on the wall against this warm cayenne, and I'd do teak countertops and cork on the floor—very soft and warm to bare feet."

BEVERLY ELLSLEY

BENJAMIN MOORE | GOLDEN HONEY 297

"Kitchens often have so little wall space you have to make the color count. This is sunshine in a can. I like a yellow with a little bit of brown in it, as opposed to a yellow with green. Looks wonderful with wood."

JOANNE HUDSON

SHERWIN-WILLIAMS | WHOLE WHEAT SW6121

"It's the color of golden brown sugar. Very appetizing, with a lot of warmth. I'd use it on the walls with white trim, and custard-colored cabinets."

MARK CUTLER

FINE PAINTS OF EUROPE | P11130

"It's an incredibly complex color, a weird combination of yellow and green with this red undertone. Beautiful."

Thomas Jayne will study how a color looks in every light, even in corners where it intensifies. He calls it the reverberating effect. This stone color is easy on the eyes and authentic to the period of the old house.

THOMAS JAYNE
BENJAMIN MOORE | SCARECROW 1041

PHILIP GORRIVAN
BENJAMIN MOORE | RAZZLE DAZZLE 1348

"Pick one wall. Apply two coats of Rust-Oleum Magnetic primer, paint it this yummy raspberry color, and then put up your children's artwork, school schedules, and birthday invites with magnets."

BARCLAY BUTERA
RALPH LAUREN PAINT | CREAM STONE UL54 (TOP)
| WEATHERED BROWN UL44 (BOTTOM)

"Paint your cabinets Cream Stone, a muted off-white, more gray than yellow. Then use rich, taupey Weathered Brown on the walls for contrast. It makes the kitchen a little more masculine, more sophisticated."

Benjamin Moore's Scarecrow gives a new kitchen wing designed by Thomas Jayne and architect Peter Pennoyer a strong visual link to the 18th-century Virginia home it serves. Benjamin Moore White Dove lifts the raftered ceiling, keeping the mood open and airy.

One red wall gives a large, streamlined kitchen just the right amount of warmth without overpowering the space.

AMANDA KEYSER

BENJAMIN MOORE | MERLOT RED 2006-10

A wall painted Merlot sets off white dishware salvaged from a grand seaside hotel in France that was torn down. The kitchen was designed to keep several family cooks from bumping elbows.

ANN MCGUIRE

VALSPAR | SPRING SQUASH 2008-1B

"You're taking a chance with orange, but it can be fabulous. It's playful during the day for kids doing projects, and at night, with the lamps lit, it glows. Start with one wall—that may be enough."

SANDRA NUNNERLEY

BENJAMIN MOORE | WOLF GRAY 2127-40

"I'm so tired of all those off-white cabinets. I'd paint them this dark Swedish gray-blue and make the whole room very Gustavian, with chalky white walls, Carrara marble countertops, and stainless-steel appliances."

JASON BELL

PRATT & LAMBERT | TAMPICO 1411

"In an old kitchen where everything was mismatched shades of white, we needed a distraction. So we painted just the doors, not the frames, of the cabinets this teal green aquamarine and replaced the cheap white plastic knobs with vintage hardware."

MICK DE GIULIO

BENJAMIN MOORE | GREAT BARRINGTON GREEN HC-122

"Especially in a small kitchen, people don't think of dark colors as an option. This is a lovely gray-green, not too dark and very soft, like moss."

WELCOMING BATHROOMS

Whether your style is ready-set-go or long soaks in the tub, these designers will bathe you in just the right color.

Every room deserves one dramatic element, like the oversized mirror hanging over the freestanding tub in this bathroom designed by Michael Smith. To heighten the effect of an old boat window, he placed the mirror against a wall painted a cotton candy blue. The overall effect is a cheery effervescence.

MICHAEL SMITH
PRATT & LAMBERT | COOS BAY 19-31

ANNE CARSON
BENJAMIN MOORE | BRILLIANT WHITE

"In a bathroom, there's nothing better than clean, fresh, pure white. This is a very clear, soothing white, not too bright and not too creamy. You never get tired of it, it never looks dated, and you can easily change the look by changing the artwork."

ATHALIE DERSE

PRATT & LAMBERT | ANTIQUE WHITE 2207

"I want a color that's subtle and refreshing at the same time. This looks like an old celadon that would have been popular back in the 1940s. First thing in the morning, I don't want anything jolting."

MICHAEL FORMICA

BENJAMIN MOORE | CALIFORNIA BLUE 2060-20

"It's a strange color, sort of an old-fashioned blue-print blue. I actually like dark bathrooms with very controlled artificial light. I think dark walls are sexy."

RONALD BRICKE

PRATT & LAMBERT | AUTUMN CROCUS 1141

"Imagine waking up and walking into the brightest, sunniest day. This is a bright lavender blue, moderately intense, very cheerful. Some people will say, 'Oh, I don't like lavender,' but this is clean, fresh—guaranteed to perk you up."

DAVID MANN

RALPH LAUREN PAINT | ARCHITECTURAL CREAM UL 55

"This is kind of a pale khaki gray. It approximates the kind of light you get on a cloudy day, which makes all the other colors around look deep and true, more intense."

CHAD EISNER
PRATT & LAMBERT | SOLITARY 19-29 (TOP)

| SILVER BIRCH 18-31 (BOTTOM)

In this master bathroom, Chad Eisner used a muted olive green to lend weight to the wainscoting and added contrast by painting the walls above a soft sand color. Both colors beautifully complement the elegant sink fixtures and pedestal table.

ROBIN BELL

FARROW & BALL | DIMITY 2008

"This is a beautiful, cloudlike off-white with just the right amount of pink in it, so people look nice—but not so flattering that you walk out the door thinking you look terrific when you really don't."

JARRETT HEDBORG

BENJAMIN MOORE | TANGERINE DREAM 2012-30

"It ain't white, honey. It's a wonderful, glowing Luis Barragán color, an orange that doesn't look silly. The dirty little secret about these big white California Spanish houses is that inside they feel dark and gray. This will make you look 10 years younger."

THAD HAYES

DONALD KAUFMAN COLOR COLLECTION | DKC-64

"It's a dark gray-brown-green, you name it, it's in there. It's almost like a clay mud color—really rich and really beautiful. Very dramatic with dark or light stone and nickel fixtures."

BARBARA SALLICK

BENJAMIN MOORE | SILVER SATIN OC-26

"White is the color of health and hygiene. It has to be the right white, something soft and warm that can complement marble, tile, porcelain, metal."

SUSAN FERRIER
BENJAMIN MOORE | CARRINGTON BEIGE HC-93 (TOP)
SHERWIN-WILLIAMS | BRAINSTORM BRONZE 7033 (BOTTOM)
Susan Ferrier used Carrington Beige, a sort of pebbly taupe, on
the walls of this luxurious master bathroom. A framing effect
is created using Brainstorm Bronze on the French doors looking
out onto a lovely garden.

STEPHANIE STOKES

BENJAMIN MOORE | FRESH DEW 435

"This is in the mint, pine family. It's a pale wash of green that reminds me of the water off Corsica in the summer. Since I spend a lot of time soaking in my Jacuzzi, I can't imagine anything better."

PRISCILLA ULMANN

FARROW & BALL | YELLOW GROUND 218

"This is a rich egg-yolk yellow, a classic English color. I used it in my own bathroom, which doesn't have any windows, and it brings in the sunlight that's not there."

BETSY BROWN

PRATT & LAMBERT | WENDIGO 2293

"This is really, really dark, almost black. It's not a color that introduces anything—you're barely aware of it at all, you just see what's in the room."

RALPH HARVARD

PRATT & LAMBERT | PELHAM GRAY LIGHT CW-819

"It's a very evasive gray from the Colonial Williamsburg line that changes color in different lights. I hate to call it a gray, because people think of gray as chilly, and this is very warm. It can look 1930s chic or 1810 countrified or 21st-century cool."

ELEGANCE
IN DINING

The dining room is the ebullient heart of any home. It can be a feast for the eyes—or a convivial backdrop for conversation. Before you set the table, let color set your dining room's mood.

"We chose a dark green for the dining room walls, which is complementary to the red kitchen cabinets. When you have a deep, rich color like that on the walls, with crisp white moldings, you don't need elaborate window treatments."

EMILY O'KEEFE
RALPH LAUREN PAINT | MASTER ROOM VM99

CHARLOTTE MOSS

FARROW & BALL | BREAKFAST ROOM GREEN 81

"When you're eating, you want a space that feels fresh, and green reads fresh to me. This is a crisp celadon. With white linens on a wooden table, it reminds me of eating outdoors. I adore eating outdoors. Everything tastes better—even my cooking!"

ARTHUR DUNNAM

BENJAMIN MOORE | BRANCHPORT BROWN HC-72

"It's a very dark chocolate brown with a bit of red in it, so there's a warm aspect to it that makes people look good. In high gloss, it really sparkles with candlelight. I think chocolate brown particularly suits a city dining room."

CELERIE KEMBLE

FARROW & BALL | MERE GREEN 219

"This is the missing jewel tone we get only in peacock feathers. It's rich and still playful—it can be a formal or sort of decadent color, and it looks beautiful with accents of white lacquer or dark wood."

JEFFREY BILHUBER

BENJAMIN MOORE | WISPY GREEN 414

"A pale, yellow-based spring green is dazzling to the complexion. Greens bring out the pink. Just think what haricots verts do for a lamb chop. It's the perfect foil."

BARCLAY BUTERA

RALPH LAUREN PAINT | CALYPSO VM138

"It's a blue with a certain nobility, something you would have seen in a colonial house in Williamsburg. But it's also a casual and comfortable color. A dining room should be approachable."

MARIETTE HIMES GOMEZ

BENJAMIN MOORE | SAGE TINT 458

"It's kind of robin's egg blue, and with mahogany furniture and neutral upholstery, it looks great. I see dining rooms as mostly evening rooms, and this has life to it. It's very soothing."

The ceiling of this Billy Haines dining room is painted with Farrow & Ball's Babouche 223 (page 155), the moldings with Pointing 2003 (page 24), and the walls with Benjamin Moore's Orange Parrot 2169-20.

MARTYN LAWRENCE-BULLARD
BENJAMIN MOORE | ORANGE PARROT 2169-20

"It's very close to a color in a 1940s Billy Haines house I restored in Beverly Hills. I love pairing it with yellow on the ceilings and ivory crown moldings like he did. Doesn't it sound wild? It's a really exotic fun orange that creates drama, yet lets you know the inhabitant is very playful."

TOM SCHEERER

BENJAMIN MOORE | CHOCOLATE CANDY BROWN 2107-10
(TOP)
| ATRIUM WHITE INTERIOR ROOM
(BOTTOM)

This turn-of-the-century dining room serves as a major
household thoroughfare, which presented designer Tom
Scheerer with a challenge. He decided to use color to
create a sense of intimacy, painting the walls a deep
chocolate brown. Paired with a cool white ceiling and
crisp trim, the combination gives the spacious room a
casual warmth.

COLIN COWIE

BENJAMIN MOORE | SHELBURNE BUFF HC-28

"This is a wonderful oatmeal, camel color. The gold hue makes everybody look like they just came back from somewhere fabulous."

MICHAEL BERMAN

RALPH LAUREN PAINT | DESERT BOOT TH35

"Like a blanket of velvet that wraps the walls—it's a really saturated rich brown, very deep, almost aubergine. It has the feeling of the background in an 18th-century portrait."

BRET WITKE

BENJAMIN MOORE | POWDER SAND 2151-70

"There's a paleness to it but also a warmth. It's like a blank canvas, so anyone who sits in front of it, or any food, any color, looks really attractive—amazing, in fact. Everything pops. The dining room is all about the table and the people sitting at it."

T. KELLER DONOVAN

BENJAMIN MOORE | BROWN SUGAR 2112-20

"If you are a chocoholic like me, you just walk in and get hungry. It's a really rich, deep, milk-chocolatey color, and we did white brackets with white vases all over the walls."

SOFT BEDROOMS

It's the room we see first thing in the morning and last thing at night. We want the colors in our bedroom to be restful and restorative, tranquil and cheerful. And with these colors, that's exactly how you feel.

"You know how some people are not comfortable with silence — they have to fill it up with words? The same can be said for a house. Some people think it has to be filled with stuff to be beautiful. It doesn't. I used color only to set a mood, not as a statement. I like to keep the background simple."

KAY DOUGLASS
BENJAMIN MOORE | SEAPEARL OC-19

WALDO FERNANDEZ
BENJAMIN MOORE | HOLIDAY WREATH 447
This color reminds designer Waldo Fernandez of the color
of wet stone, a cool kind of gray-green, like slate after a
summer rain. It provides an effective backdrop for a series
of framed nature studies that he arranged on the walls of
his son's bedroom.

MARIO BUATTA

BENJAMIN MOORE | MISTY LILAC 2071-70

"What you want is anything that makes a woman look more beautiful. Lavender is great for blondes or brunettes and very pretty with blue-and-white fabric. Just don't tell your husband it's lavender."

T. KELLER DONOVAN

FARROW & BALL | BORROWED LIGHT 235

"The name says it all. It's the palest blue that they make, and it just shimmers. When you walk into a room with white woodwork and this pale blue, you think you're in heaven. My painter went home and told his wife about it, so you know you've got a winner."

ALESSANDRA BRANCA

PRATT & LAMBERT | AVOINE DE MER 17-26

"It's green, somewhere between apple and moss, and it's like waking up in spring every morning."

BIRCH COFFEY

BENJAMIN MOORE | PALE MOON OC-108

"Nothing is more of a turn-on than Champagne, and this is that same uplifting kind of inviting color. In the evening, it looks very warm and rich, and in the morning, there's a happy mood about it."

SUZANNE RHEINSTEIN

RALPH LAUREN PAINT | CRESTED BUTTE NA40

"It's the color of stones under water—relatively dark, but very warm and nuanced. It's wonderful to have a dark bedroom. Aren't there a few people who like to use this room for sleeping?"

SHEILA BRIDGES

FARROW & BALL | GREEN BLUE 84

"It's my two favorite colors mixed together. Soft, but with a lot of vibrancy. Greens and blues are known for their relaxing effect."

BRIAN MCCARTHY

BENJAMIN MOORE | CAYMAN BLUE 2060-50

"I happen to love this color. I've mixed it with black-and-white photography and some pretty serious Empire furniture, and it's really fabulous."

CHARLOTTE MOSS

BENJAMIN MOORE | BLANCHED CORAL 886

"It's a pale, pale, pale, almost fleshy pink, but on the pink side rather than the beige side. It's feminine and soft. It's almost like you've got a little glow in your cheeks. That's what you want in the morning when you wake up and have no makeup on. Green was not going to work for me."

MARSHALL WATSON

DONALD KAUFMAN COLOR COLLECTION | DKC-37

"What I like about Donald Kaufman paints is that they're indescribable. This particular shade has green and blue in it, and brown and gray. A February sea blue. I always use it in flat, so it has this rich velvety quality, like soft moonlight."

DD ALLEN

C2 | BELLA DONNA C2-316 W

"It's a smoky, purply mauve, the color of the sky at sunset. It's a soothing, relaxing, moody color that looks beautiful with raspberry curtains, mauve bedding, and gray flannel carpet."

KATHRYN M. IRELAND

FARROW & BALL | CITRON 74

"It reminds me of the sunflowers that surround my house in France. It's bright, cheerful. Even when it's dark, it's always going to be happy."

MILES REDD

BENJAMIN MOORE | BIRD'S EGG 2051-60

"My bedroom is painted a very pale blue, with touches of silver gray and coral. I'm a Pisces, and I'm always totally gravitating to water and cool colors."

SUZANNE KASLER

GLIDDEN | LIMOGES BLUE 30BG56/045

Suzanne Kasler dreamed up a cool blue bedroom that is
the epitome of tranquillity. The black-lacquered bed gives
the classic backdrop a contemporary edge.

"I did this room for a 14-year-old who's now in college," says designer Natasha Baradaran, "and she asked her mother if I could decorate her dorm room the same way. That was a big compliment."

INVITING
CHILDREN'S ROOMS

Kids go through phases in the blink of an eye, so opt for a color that won't get tossed out with the wooden blocks. The vivid hues on the following pages never grow old.

"There are a lot of vibrant colors in this room, but the pale green on the walls—like mint icing on a cupcake—is the one that sticks with you. It calms down the bright upholstery and feels cool and soothing."

NATASHA BARADARAN
DUNN-EDWARDS | SOFT MINT DE5686

TRACEY PRUZAN
BENJAMIN MOORE | ATRIUM WHITE 79

"My daughter thinks she has a pink room, but the walls are actually white, with a pink cast. Done in an eggshell finish they reflect her pink shag rug and the pink fabrics. But down the line, she could simply switch out the rug and accessories to achieve a completely different look. It gives her more flexibility to grow into her room."

TIMOTHY WHEALON
BENJAMIN MOORE | NORTHERN AIR 1676

"It's funny how kids attach themselves to color. This four-year-old boy wanted blue, and I chose a saturated blue with a bit of sky and smoke in it, so it had some sophistication. Then we chose furniture to grow into—a Moroccan rug, African textiles in browns and tans and whites, a Lucite desk chair. Five years later, it still works."

OPPOSITE PAGE:

For a client's son who was fascinated with pirates, **Mica Ertegun** painted the walls of his room a cool **Caribbean** blue. The boatshaped bed and witty nautical sconces extended the oceangoing theme.

MICA ERTEGUN
BENJAMIN MOORE | OCEAN BREEZE 2058-60

KATIE RIDDER
FARROW & BALL | FARROW'S CREAM 67

"This is a dirty buttercup yellow with a little green in it, a good tone-down color for all the chaos that comes with a kid's room. It's a neutral backdrop, so the child gets to bring in his own personality. The fabrics you choose will make it masculine or feminine, and they can change as the child gets older. I love the sculptural quality of those iron beds—grown-up enough to work when this transitions into a guest room."

STEPHEN SAINT-ONGE

MYTHIC PAINT | PEBBLE BEACH 167-2

"Anything that reminds me of walking along a beach is a great starting point. A classic sand color like this, neutral enough to work over several years, acts as a foundation; the details can change as the child starts exploring his or her own personal style. It looks sunny with natural light streaming in, and then in the evening it's comfortable and warm. Plus, it's nontoxic and as a parent myself, that's very important."

SARA STORY

FARROW & BALL | CALAMINE 230

"This could go a long way because it's not the usual pink. It has a touch of gray, which makes it more interesting. Start out with white trim and ballerina artwork. Then switch to gray trim and contemporary photography. It could look very Christian Dior. Or Marie Antoinette, with playful pistachio or pale blue accents. If you want to rock out, accent it with chartreuse, red, or black."

ASHLEY WHITTAKER
BENJAMIN MOORE | MOUNTAIN MIST 868

Ashley Whittaker wanted the bedroom for her client's college-age daughter to feel sophisticated, but still youthful and feminine. She chose a tranquil blue for the walls, the added accents of lavender, navy, and turquoise. They're colors "that say 'girl' without screaming 'girly girl,'" explains the designer.

LESLIE MAY
BENJAMIN MOORE | SPRING LILAC 1388

"Purple is the favorite color of this five-year-old girl.
But when the princess dolls are packed away, this
shade can look very sophisticated. We've already
picked out a black, white, and lavender Manuel
Canovas toile to go with it, when she's a teenager"

LORI FELDMAN
BENJAMIN MOORE | DOWN POUR BLUE 2063-20

"Baby blue lasts about two years, if that. So I prefer
a marine blue that doesn't go too dark. With white
trim, it's bright and energetic. When he's older,
bring in forest-green Black Watch plaid to take
it from nautical to preppy."

MICHAEL WHALEY
BENJAMIN MOORE | LAVENDER SECRET 1415

"This changes. I used it with purple and pale
green, which made the walls very lavender.
Once the girl was in high school we redid the
room with John Robshaw prints and it took on
an upbeat Moroccan look."

CHAPTER

2

COLORS
TO BRIGHTEN
YOUR DAY

The shell-splashed fabric on the
armchair and bed is **Concarneau**
from **Pierre Frey**.

COLORS THAT MAKE YOU FEEL GOOD

There's nothing more uplifting than clear yellow, real red, relaxing blue. Here are twelve shades sure to make you smile.

This blue is cool, restful—there's a sense of depressuring. This guest room reflects a Paula Perlini truism: "Everyone loves blue and white."

PAULA PERLINI

BENJAMIN MOORE | RIVIERA AZURE 822

"It's a funny combination of pink and red and coral. Colors in that range are very stimulating—good for conversation; they keep people's minds going. It looks luscious in a satin finish."

LIBBY CAMERON

BENJAMIN MOORE | MILANO RED 1313

ROBERT STILIN

FARROW & BALL | COOKING APPLE GREEN 32

"I'm in my office looking out at this field where horses graze, and the sun has turned the grass this rich, vibrant yellowy green, and it just looks so happy."

MARY DOUGLAS DRYSDALE

BENJAMIN MOORE | JAMAICAN AQUA 2048-60

"This is a pale teal, a really lovely neoclassical color that goes with high heels and beautiful earrings and sixteen sets of china."

JOHN YUNIS

FINE PAINTS OF EUROPE | SUNNYSIDE LANE 7014T

"It's hard to get yellow right—usually it's too green or too red or too muddy. But this is nice and clear, without being shrill. If it's too vivid, it's like living in an omelet."

In this living room, Libby Cameron uses white to cool down the red. The chair is painted in ½ Bright White and ½ Linen White, both by Benjamin Moore.

LEE MELAHN

VALSPAR | WOODLAWN SILVER BROOK 5001-1B

"This is like an exhalation, a soothing breath that allows the mind and body to relax. It's the color of the sky in that moment of silence before a storm—a soft gray with a hint of blue and silver."

OPPOSITE PAGE :

The dark and cozy taupe walls of this library are the perfect backdrop for the exotic and colorful Indian- and Asian-inspired fabrics, rugs and throw pillows in this cozy library by Amanda Kyser.

AMANDA KYSER
BENJAMIN MOORE | DEEP TAUPE 2111-10

DAVID MITCHELL
BENJAMIN MOORE | SWEET DREAMS 847

"Sweet Dreams is like a hug. I know that sounds sappy, but this is the perfect nice, comfortable blue, with just enough gray, and just enough robin's egg, and just enough teal. Paint any room with this, and it becomes the happiest room in your house—but not in a clownish, perky way. My kind of happiness means serenity and atmosphere."

SARA BENGUR
DONALD KAUFMAN COLOR COLLECTION | DKC-30

"It's the color of afternoon light—that end-of-the-day moment when it feels warm and mellow and everything has a glow. I'm thinking some beautiful house on the Mediterranean, and we're sitting outside and eating figs with a bottle of white wine."

MATTHEW PATRICK SMYTH
PRATT & LAMBERT | VINTAGE CLARET 1013

"This is a real red, a true red that's not trying to be anything else but red. I used it in my living room, and it never fails to get a reaction. I once had someone look at the color and say, 'I wish I could go through life with these walls behind me.'"

SUSAN ZISES GREEN
DURON MOUNT VERNON ESTATE OF COLOURS | LEAMON SIRRUP DMV070

"This is the color of a pistachio nut—a clear, sharp yellow-green with no sadness in it at all. I used it in a show house for Kips Bay, and there wasn't a person who came in who did not smile."

THOMAS GUNKELMAN
BENJAMIN MOORE | BLEEKER BEIGE HC-80

"This isn't beige the way we think of beige—so boring. This has warmth and depth. It's a very sophisticated color that makes me feel good and I know I look good against it."

In this dining alcove by **Peter Vaughn**, the high-gloss floor—painted **Benjamin Moore's Mauve Bauhaus 1407**—is a darker version of the lavender walls.

PETER VAUGHN
BENJAMIN MOORE | SPRING IRIS 1402

"I started out as a painter, and I'd always add purple to other colors to give them depth and richness. Lavender reflects light well, which is why you see it all over Scandinavia. In the depth of winter, it's a very cheerful color to walk into."

The bedroom by architect **David Mann** is a cocoon of shimmering silver with
rich tones and sophisticated fabrics.

MODERN TONES

It's more than a style. It's a state of mind, which makes these colors very personal.

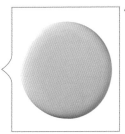

"I'm drawn to bright, shiny things, and this is a metallic paint that's not overbearing. It has a subtle luster that gives depth to the walls. I like it tone-on-tone with other silver-grays, or with black and steely blues. It's soothing in bedrooms and has a more finished effect than a typical painted wall, which makes it a cost-effective alternative to upholstery or wallpaper."

DAVID MANN
MODERN MASTERS | PLATINUM ME 591

ALEXANDRA CHAMPALIMAUD

SHERWIN-WILLIAMS | MORNING GLORY SW 6971

"I like colors that trigger emotions in people. This saturated Prussian blue-purple practically pulsates with drama and will intensify the impact of your décor. Try it in a foyer where it invites you in and acts as a decompression chamber from the outside world."

KIRSTEN BRANT

BENJAMIN MOORE | PASSION PLUM 2073-30

"There's something mysterious and magical about purple. A den or a library or a family room—where you might traditionally go to a sage green or a blood red—would feel more modern in this shade, which is like the inside of a pansy. And darker colors are always sexy, because they warm things up and make everyone look better."

SARA STORY

PRATT & LAMBERT | DARK TEAL 21-16

"Jewel tones are so now—sapphire blues, emerald greens, and this teal that's right in the middle. The peacock hues are vibrant and full of energy. Try this with black lacquered furniture, burnished brass. Luxurious in a dining room, or very crisp and current as an accent wall in a living room."

KRIM DANZINGER
GLIDDEN | CLEAR BLUE SKY GLB15
"This is a clean, clear blue that suggests sky and air and a new kind of energy. It feels pure and trustworthy. The color doesn't come at you—it recedes, which gives a room a nice sensation of openness. Just looking at it gives me the confidence to feel I can make a fresh start."

JOHN BARMAN
FARROW & BALL | CHARLOTTE'S LOCKS 268
"It's new and a little different—not quite orange and not quite red. More of a persimmon. It feels warm and inviting when you come in from the cold, and if there's a little mess in the mudroom, you don't notice because you're so surprised by this rich, exciting color. We even painted the moldings and doors to make it more intense."

WILLIAM SOFIELD

PAPERS AND PAINTS | PERSIAN YELLOW HC15

"In the south drawing room of Sir John Soane's Museum in London, the walls are painted a sulfurous, sun-drenched yellow that is absolutely electric. I'm always staggered by how modern and voluptuous it feels. I would use it in dim back bedrooms or north-facing rooms."

JAY JEFFERS

BENJAMIN MOORE | CHEATING HEART 1617

"If you had told me three years ago that I was going to be using gray in every project, I would have said, 'No way.' But the switch for me was realizing how versatile it could be. You can start with this soft charcoal gray and then bring in any accent tone— apricot, chartreuse, yellow, blue."

STEVEN GAMBREL

PANTONE | CITRONELLE 15-0548

"This feels like nature at its sharpest, most vivid moment. I'd use it in a room between rooms—a bar, vestibule, or butler's pantry. Then it becomes a surprise."

YOUNG HUH
FARROW & BALL | TERESA'S GREEN 236
"Designer Young Huh used a muted mint green to give a contemporary touch to the old-fashioned country kitchen his clients requested. "We got unfinished cabinets and painted them because they didn't want that baked-on factory finish. The blue-green is at once retro and fresh.""

AMY LAU
BENJAMIN MOORE | GOSSAMER BLUE 2123-40

"This has elements of silver, green, gray, and blue. It's complex, and that's what makes it feel modern. In the evening, it shimmers in the light and makes dark wood furniture look great. I'd layer the same color in varying textures—silk, velvet, mohair—throughout the room."

ROB STUART
GLIDDEN | ANTIQUE SLIVER GLN51

"My new favorite color is this silvery gray. It washes the room in an icy haze, like moonlight on the snow in mid-winter. It has this hush about it that makes it the perfect neutral. It doesn't collide with anything—it just falls away, like a shadow."

TIM CAMPBELL
BENJAMIN MOORE | ELECTRIC ORANGE 2015-10

"I love opinionated colors that instantly evoke a mood and revive the sense. This orange reminds me of the souk in Marrakech—the pungent smell of exotic spices, animated bartering, storytellers, snake charmers."

Amanda Kyser painted the mid-century chair at the foot of the staircase the same dramatic color used on the wall.

ADVENTUROUS REDS

Subtlety is not red's calling card. There are plenty of other colors for that. We look to this life force to be rich and vital—assertive enough to add some needed spark to a scene without screaming.

"We painted the front hall stairwell the color of old Chinese lacquer. We painted it with old-fashioned enamel, too, the kind that takes three days to dry, and then I picked up that color throughout the house."

AMANDA KYSER

BENJAMIN MOORE | MERLOT RED 2006-10

ELDON WONG

BENJAMIN MOORE | REDSTONE 2009-10

Small dose, big impact: Eldon Wong used a rich saturated red on the back interior of the cupboard built into the dining room wall of this 18th-century stone house. The brilliant color perfectly accents a 1950s Rosenthal china service by Raymond Loewy.

SUZANNE KASLER
RALPH LAUREN PAINT | DRESSAGE RED TH41

"When I look for red, I want a pure, true red, like the color in the American flag. Ralph Lauren does absolutely the best. It's the essence of red. It makes me think of boating or polo."

DAVID EASTON
FARROW & BALL | BLAZER 212

"It's exciting and it has a historical reference: the Greek vases, the palace at Knossos, and all that business. I love red, always have, always will. Either you like steak or you like hamburgers."

MARIO BUATTA
BENJAMIN MOORE | MERLOT RED 2006-10

"I like a touch of red in every room—it brings life, like red lips on a woman. I did an entire library in Merlot. It looked great."

ALISON SPEAR
BENJAMIN MOORE | RUBY RED 2001-10

"Red is a neutral for me. Like red nail polish, it's classic. It goes with everything. I actually had that Coco Chanel red lacquer nail polish matched, and I painted the floors of my living and dining rooms with it. They're the most fun floors I've ever had."

"All my life I've pursued the perfect red. I can never get painters to mix it for me. It's exactly as if I'd said 'I want Rococo with a spot of Gothic in it and a bit of Buddhist temple'—they have no idea what I'm talking about."

DIANA VREELAND
BENJAMIN MOORE RED 2000-10

PETER DUNHAM

PRATT & LAMBERT | PAGODA RED 5-15

"It's not too orange, not too blue—it looks like an antique red, a Pompeian red. I used it in a bathroom with white Carrara marble floors from a monastery. It made them sing. Almost everything looks good with it."

JOE NYE

PORTOLA PAINTS | PAPRIKA 013

"This paint has a strié effect, very obvious brush marks that appear as it dries. It can take a drab space and give it dignity. Paprika is warm, welcoming, and slightly dramatic—it makes food look great, people look great, candlelight look great."

There's no red room as famous as Diana Vreeland's "garden in hell" by Billy Baldwin. The Bracquenié chintz, Le Grand Arbre, is available to the trade from Pierre Frey. Nobody knows exactly what red her room was, but we found a good match in Benjamin Moore Red.

SUZANNE KASLER

GLIDDEN | CHECKERBERRY 32RR50/260

"It's daring, but everyone loves it—a rich peony pink that doesn't look at all little girl–ish. The pink accentuates this smaller area and makes it very cozy. It is important, though, when you use a bold color like this, that you make sure it has enough depth in it. Colors that have no depth are oddly fluorescent. They leap out at you, rather than pull you in."

ELISSA CULLMAN
BENJAMIN MOORE | SANGRIA 2006-20

"Lately I'm on this anti-completely-neutral kick. You have to have some seasoning in your rooms. Sangria is a good, universal-donor red—not too blue, not too orange, not too dark."

RODERICK SHADE
BENJAMIN MOORE | MILLION DOLLAR RED 2003-10

"It's a true, deep red. I like the temperature of it: it's a bit cooler. But a little red goes a long way. It's good in areas where you don't spend much time or in boring areas that need a strong burst of color."

WILLIAM DIAMOND AND ANTHONY BARATTA
RALPH LAUREN PAINT | LATTICE RED IB57

"Red never goes out of style. It's full of life—always fresh, always fun to wake up to. We go for reds with less blue in them and more orange because they're happier to live with."

ALEXA HAMPTON
BENJAMIN MOORE | TUCSON RED 1300

"This is a very bricky red. I prefer the warmth of earth tones to the bluer reds, which are trickier—some make me think of nail polish. I'm fine with bluer reds on my toes, but not necessarily on my walls."

THE MOST
FLATTERING PINKS

Think pink is too sweet? It's time to take another look. This irrepressible color can be sophisticated, energizing, soothing, inviting—and surprisingly pleasing to men.

"Wherever you see this color, you instantly equate it with a passion for life. It's a timeless pink, believe it or not. The Venetians and Moroccans have used it for centuries!"

WINDSOR SMITH

BENJAMIN MOORE | PINK BEGONIA 2078-50

ALEXA HAMPTON

BENJAMIN MOORE | LOVE & HAPPINESS 1191

"This is a ballet-slipper pink with a hint of beige, which keeps it from looking too sweet. When picking a pink, always go to the top of the card and get the palest version of what you're dreaming of, because even if it looks subtle on the chip, it won't be so subtle on the wall."

....

JACKIE TERRELL

VALSPAR | PARIS PINK MS037

"I like using pink in an unexpected place like a kitchen or an entryway. It's flattering and familiar. We think of pink as an old lady color, but it can be very young if used the right way—with touches of cobalt blue, red, orange, or green."

....

KELLY WEARSTLER

PRATT & LAMBERT | CORAL PINK 2-8

"Pink all by itself can be perceived as feminine, but what you pair it with makes all the difference. Think of a man in a black suit with a pink shirt and tie, or plopping a pink sofa into a listless beige room. Pink is suddenly daring and electric. The right shade of pink can energize any space."

PHOEBE HOWARD

SHERWIN-WILLIAMS | WHITE DOGWOOD SW 6315

"I love pink. It makes me feel warm and fuzzy. I just want to slip on a ruffly boudoir jacket and lean back into the pillow and eat chocolate. This pink is very soft and feminine, but it's not sticky. Pair it with white or metallic surfaces to make it ethereal and inviting."

"Orchid pink is wildly lush and not at all juvenile. This room feels almost aromatic, redolent of complex perfume. Pink conjures love, embraces, and kisses."

MARCY MASTERSON

SYDNEY HARBOUR PAINT COMPANY | PRISCILLA

"This is a pulsing hot pink. I would do it with white trim and ebonized black floors, a white Moroccan rug, shades of indigo on the furniture. Or maybe saffron and tangerine. You walk in and feel incredibly happy."

JENNIFER GARRIGUES

BENJAMIN MOORE | WHEATBERRY 2099-70

"It's just a whisper of pink. Very, very pretty—but not sweet. Those candy-sweet pinks are not my cup of tea. This has a teeny bit of brown in it. It's one of those dirty colors that look as if they've been around for a while, which I like. In a living room, it would be very smart with tobacco and white, or citrus green, or a very pale turquoise."

THOMAS JAYNE

BENJAMIN MOORE | PALE PINK SATIN 008

"I like looking at old-fashioned color schemes, and there's a lot of pink in 18th-and 19th-century decoration. You see this soft pink in old Sèvres porcelain. It has a slightly yellow cast, which makes it warmer and more flattering. Everyone looks good against it."

"**We've always been partial to pink. This is a clear, clean color that looks new and fresh. It's softer than red, yet just as warm.**"

WILLIAM DIAMOND AND ANTHONY BARATTA

PITTSBURGH PAINTS | ROSE FANTASY 136-4

ROBIN BELL

BENJAMIN MOORE | OLD COUNTRY OC-76

"I'll often look at the French mats on old drawings for ideas, because the colors they used are never obvious—like this dusty pink. It has a little yellow and a bit of brown in it. It's the color of the pink sand in the Bahamas. I used it in a guest bedroom to convey a sense of peace and tranquility."

CHARLOTTE MOSS

PANTONE | 705-C

"This pale pink reminds me of opals and pears, Jean Harlow and silk charmeuse, 'New Dawn' roses, and a baby's rosy cheeks. Who wouldn't want a perpetual glow like that? When it comes to decorating, it's perfect with black and white and everything in between. And real men do like pink—they just might not admit it at first!"

OPPOSITE PAGE :

"This is a color you'd see in Rome. It's a more ancient pink with a lot of terra-cotta in it. Think of an old Italian villa that has been baking in the sun for years. It just glows. I used it in this library in high gloss—brushed, not rolled—because then it glows that much more."

KATIE RIDDER

FARROW & BALL | RED EARTH 64

LIBBY CAMERON

BENJAMIN MOORE | CAT'S MEOW 1332

"This really does look like the inside of a mouse's ear. It's a good clear pink that has very little blue in it, so it doesn't turn cold. Pink is a color with a lot of animation. There's almost a fey quality to it. You could bring in apple green or bachelor-button blue or stay with white. I once did a living room in pink and white and beige, like a conch shell."

FAVORITE GREENS

Nature's best-loved color makes a gorgeous backdrop for an infinite variety of hues, much as foliage throws a flower into high relief. Grass, lichen, palest fern—these sensuous shades fire the imaginations of the following 15 designers.

"Both my office and my library are painted in this mossy, olivey green. It works like a neutral, allowing me to play around with stronger, sharper colors like shocking pink, apple green, and chromium yellow. It's a fabulous background for artwork as well."

BUNNY WILLIAMS

BENJAMIN MOORE | CLEVELAND GREEN 1525

ELLEN KENNON
FULL SPECTRUM PAINTS | LICHEN
"Lichen is that silvery gray-green with blue undertones that
you see everywhere in Louisiana, from tree bark to tomb-
stones. It's both soothing and grounding. I use some sort
of green in almost every project because I think it's the
most healing color."

THOMAS O'BRIEN
DONALD KAUFMAN COLOR | DKC-29

"This is by far my favorite. See how it's incredibly rich with pigment? I think of it as the most lively pale green, but it also goes blue and gray. It behaves in this completely natural way with light and can appear so different in different settings."

. . . .

BARBARA BARRY
BENJAMIN MOORE | CYPRESS GREEN 509

"Born and raised in California, I always grew up with some shade of green outside my window. I suspect that's why it's a defining color for me. This is my murky, pond-scum green. Cagey in its neutrality, it seems to go with almost everything. I love how it sets off other colors, like a soft celadon or a saturated orange."

. . . .

SUZANNE TUCKER
GLIDDEN | THYME 70YY 46/160

"This is very organic, with a bit of dustiness to it. It's a surprisingly versatile neutral. I would balance the coolness of the green with golden yellow and rose. It would also work beautifully with brown bark colors or blue—colors you would find next to it in nature."

"I love mixing greens," says Meg Braff. This butler's pantry, painted the lush, leafy shade of a woodland, "is a little green jewel box," the designer says. The unlacquered brass hardward will "eventually weather to look a little green itself."

MEG BRAFF

BENJAMIN MOORE | FOREST MOSS 2146-20

EDWARD LOBRANO

BEHR | OLIVINE 420F-5

"This green reminds me of the olive tree, a symbol of peace around the world. Maybe that's why it complements almost any other color you put with it."

MICHAEL RICHMAN

SHERWIN-WILLIAMS | GLEEFUL SW6709

"I was walking through a client's living room and said, very softly, 'Pistachio.' Instead of calling me crazy, she picked up on it immediately and we chose this vibrant green, lighter than pear but with a certain pungent quality. It elevated the whole room and made it feel more sophisticated."

WINDSOR SMITH

DUNN-EDWARDS | RIPE PEAR DE5515

"Right now I'm really into chartreuse, especially when it's mixed with all those rich hues of pink that you find only in garden roses. And porcelain blue layered on top would create a palpable tingling effect! A great paint color is never meant to stand on its own."

....

PAUL FORTUNE

DONALD KAUFMAN COLOR | DKC-26

"I bought a ranch in Ojai and painted the gates sage green to go with the California oaks. I guess most of nature is green for a reason. It's pleasing. But I've also seen this color in a St. Petersburg castle with gilt mirrors and candlelight, and in a country cottage with French printed linens. It's a universal tranquil shade."

....

KELLY WEARSTLER

PRATT & LAMBERT | SUNNY MEADOW 19-17

"Green is such an amazing, confident color. It's life-giving and it makes me think of nature, health, and vitality. This is a crisp green that would be really pretty—punk and preppy—with pink."

STEVEN GAMBREL
PANTONE | CRÈME DE MENTHE 16-5919
"An entrance hall is a great place to play with color
because you want that element of surprise. This green is
striking, and it has enough presence to glue together all
three floors of this 1800s Greenwich Village town house
as it continues up the stair hall. Colors were bolder back
then: they were meant to be seen by candlelight."

"You shouldn't use too many colors when you're working with bold shades," says Allison Paladino. For the master bedroom in a Palm Beach house, she chose a vibrant green for the walls, letting it set the tone for the linens, upholstered sofa, and artwork. Against this unified background, the dark wood bed and nightstand appear rich and elegant.

ALLISON PALADINO
BENJAMIN MOORE | MESQUITE 501

JAMIE DRAKE
BENJAMIN MOORE | SEA GLASS PT-330

"I rarely use the same color twice, to be honest, but I'm drawn to these metallic paints because they're so changeable. This green is like a wonderful pieces of glass washed up on the beach. I love the way light dances across it."

ASHLEY WHITTAKER
BENJAMIN MOORE | PEALE GREEN HC-121

"This is a real Park Avenue men's club kind of green…chesterfield sofas, leather-bound books. Dark enough to make you feel cozy, but still with a lot of life in it."

THE **BEST ORANGE**

Warm, elegant, and embracing, orange is the color of Tuscan sunsets, terra-cotta tiles, and good cognac. Try one of these unexpected shades in a dining room or library and prepare to be dazzled.

"I wanted a warm, dusty apricot for the walls of this luxurious master bath. Orange can be romantic and sexy. It makes you feel like you've just come in from the beach and your skin is glowing."

STEPHEN SHUBEL
BENJAMIN MOORE | SOFT MARIGOLD 160

MARCY MASTERSON

SYDNEY HARBOUR PAINT COMPANY | BLOOD ORANGE

"This quickens the pulse and excites the eye. It brings back the hue and the scent of blood oranges piled high in the market stalls of Tuscany. With a black-and-white floor and Benjamin Moore's Linen White trim, it would be the perfect foil for an array of drawings."

CHERYL KATZ

BENJAMIN MOORE | PALE DAFFODIL 2017-60

"This is a pale, pale orange. It's really the color of candlelight, and it does the same thing for your walls. It gives them a glow. It will turn any room into a light box. You could play off the warmth with some cool gray-blues, or if you want to bump up the volume, bring in mustard or celadon green or periwinkle."

JOHN PEIXINHO

BENJAMIN MOORE | AUDUBON RUSSET HC-51

"You can't let orange scare you. Paint this warm, bricky orange on the inside of a bookcase and it will add unexpected depth to a small space. One of the most fascinating rooms I've ever seen had ivory walls and a ceiling painted this color. Very cozy."

COURTNEY COLEMAN
CALIFORNIA PAINTS | PUMPKIN 16

"A red dining room is perfectly acceptable, so why not a deep persimmon sitting room? The color is so warm and cozy that it makes you feel as if there's a fire in the fireplace, even when there is none. They say people who choose orange are very self-confident and extroverted. For this library, we borrowed the unusual finish from the parlor of the Thomas Everard House in Colonial Williamsburg, where varnish is applied over your base paint."

CARE MALONEY

DONALD KAUFMAN COLOR | DKC-35

"This terra-cotta is earthy and elegant—how many colors can claim that combination? Dark woods look great against it, and so does art. I like it dead flat, with a white trim and black baseboards to play up that Grecian urn thing. Very Brideshead Revisited."

MARKHAM ROBERTS

BENJAMIN MOORE | CORLSBUD CANYON 074

"This color has great impact without looking like that garish NFL orange. I'd use it with ivory, black, and brown for a sophisticated classical look, or with cobalt blue, navy, and white if you want to go bolder, younger."

HEIDI BONESTEEL

PORTOLA PAINTS | SUMMER SQUASH 022

"Orange makes a room feel young, fresh, and modern. I would feel really happy in a room painted this pretty golden orange, with navy, turquoise, or pink as an accent."

HEATHER MOORE
RALPH LAUREN PAINT | CORK

"I'm not afraid of color. For this apartment living room I knew I wanted to use orangey autumnal tones, and I chose Ralph Lauren's Cork for the walls. It's a burnt umber, a saturated color that doesn't read as flat. It has more reflectivity and depth than that."

MONA ROSS BERMAN
BENJAMIN MOORE | FRESNO 020
"Orange is one of the only colors that can be sophisticated and unpretentious at the same time. The doors to the laundry room in this beach house could have been a lost opportunity—just another pair of white doors. But we felt they shouldn't be an afterthought. Painting them orange made them very visible and special. They read as art."

ANN WOLF

BENJAMIN MOORE | FIRENZE AF-225

"I'm envisioning a library or a den, an unapologetically adult room where you'd congregate at night to have drinks. I was trying to replicate the color of whiskey and chose this earthy terra-cotta with elements of yellow and gold, apricot, and peach."

ERINN VALENCICH

ACE PAINT | YUMA B21-6

"You need a little brown in your orange to keep it from getting too citrusy. This reminds me of saddle leather. I've seen it in those great Palm Desert houses, with midcentury modern furniture and a flokati rug. But I'd jazz it up with a hot pink, apple green, or peacock blue. And a heavy dose of white or cocoa brown would really soften it."

MAUREEN FOOTER

BENJAMIN MOORE | ORANGE SKY 2018-10

"This is a Veuve Clicquot orange that we used inside kitchen cabinets, for a bon vivant whose signature pour is Champagne. Coat the paint with beeswax if you want an antique look."

COLORS
FOR COZINESS

You know the kind of rooms we're talking about: warm, intimate, homey. They're decked with comfortable colors; colors that remind you of the soft gray of an old wool blanket.

In this romantic homage to the 1920s Spanish-style Mizner houses, designer Fern Santini painted new kitchen cabinets Nantucket Gray and treated them with a custom sienna glaze.

FERN SANTINI

BENJAMIN MOORE | NANTUCKET GRAY HC-111

Designer Amanda Kyser tucked a small daybed into a cozy wall alcove, then used a soothing honey brown paint on the walls to create a comfortable retreat for rest and relaxation.

AMANDA KYSER

BENJAMIN MOORE | VALLEY FORGE BROWN HC-74

MARSHALL WATSON

SHERWIN-WILLIAMS | HUMBLE GOLD SW6380

"Humble Gold has such warmth on a gray winter day. It just snuggles into you. There are so many colors in it—gold, yellow, pink, red. That little blush brings out the rosiness in your cheeks when you come in from the cold. It's not a sharp color. That's what makes it cozy and inviting."

STEPHANIE STOKES

FARROW & BALL | CLAYDON BLUE 87

"My library gets no light, so I took advantage of the disadvantage and painted it this deep blue-green. It's a restful color, kind of an ancient color. You see it in the medieval tapestries at the Cluny Museum. Now everybody gravitates to my dark, cozy room. And the color works with anything— Oriental rugs, African pillows, Islamic textiles."

TODD ROMANO

FARROW & BALL | BLAZER 212

"Red is not a color for sissies, but you can't go wrong with this good orangey red that reminds me of carved cinnabar boxes from China. It's warm and cheerful with chintz. Or add a coat of gloss for a lacquered effect and the room will feel like a glamorous jewel box."

PATRICIA HILL

DONALD KAUFMAN COLOR COLLECTION | DKC-11

"This is about atmosphere. It's a really soft shade of green—a pale, pale sage. Very soothing. It's a Donald Kaufman color, which means it will be different depending on the light, and that makes it interesting. I like it with a muted paisley or one of those tea-stained English linens made by Robert Kime or Bennison."

MICHAEL WHALEY

BENJAMIN MOORE | GARDEN CUCUMBER 644

"To me, cozy is a dark color like this green, with just a trace of blue. It's the color of the green baize door in an old English country house. Cozy needs to be small, intimate, a place where you can curl up with a drink by the fire. Dark, rich colors actually make me feel introspective. Bring in some deep wood tones and a bit of gilt for some sparkle."

FRANKLIN SALASKY

BENJAMIN MOORE | MUSTANG 2111-30

"In an all-white house, I'll often do one room, like the study or the TV room, that's a total reversal. I'll paint it very dark, like this espresso brown, so you have a completely different feeling. Darkness creates intimacy. Bring in deep blues and reds. Actually, every color looks good with it."

MICHAEL ROBERSON

BENJAMIN MOORE | POWELL BUFF HC-35

"This wonderful warm tan is almost the color of dried wheat. What makes it so pretty is the way it reacts to light. When the sun hits it, it glows, and on a rainy day it casts a nice kind of cozy warm shadow on the room. Very calming in a bedroom. Great in a sitting room with almond-colored suede or gray flannel."

JOHN SALADINO

**MARTIN SENOUR | MARKET SQUARE TAVERN
DARK GREEN CW401**

"This is a beautiful deep inky green. Use it in a
high-gloss, oil-based paint—first prep the walls
so they're absolutely smooth—and it will make
the most dismal room feel warm and rich. I call
it the poor man's paneling. Great in a library, or
an entrance hall where it would make the living
room beyond seem bigger, lighter, brighter."

TORI GOLUB

DONALD KAUFMAN COLOR COLLECTION | DKC-62

"At first glance, this is a soft grayish putty. Then its
golden undertones unfold as it catches the light
and it radiates with warmth. It's like pale ashes
with hidden embers glowing beneath them. It's an
old warmth, and the color is always changing."

CHRISTOPHER MAYA

FARROW & BALL | RECTORY RED 217

"Red is one of those colors that is inherently cozy.
But it's a difficult color to get right. Either it gets
very rusty or it becomes too saturated and bright.
But this has enough blue in it so it doesn't go into
fire-engine mode. It's a refined red. It makes you
feel special."

BARBARA WESTBROOK
BENJAMIN MOORE | WHITALL BROWN HC-69 (TOP)
| OVERCAST OC-43 (BOTTOM)
**Designer Barbara Westbrook chose a satiny brown
for the walls of this paneled study. It's a very serene
color and the off-white on the ceiling provides
a needed contrast. The sunlight adds a natural glow
throughout the room.**

MYRA HOEFER

RALPH LAUREN PAINT | CALIFORNIA POPPY GH170

"I saw Andrew Lloyd Webber's music room, and
now I want to paint everything this color. It's a
true tangerine orange, and they must have put a
squirt of burnt umber in the glaze, because it's
like a nicotine stain. It looks old and rich and
warm. The room glows. It's like having a fabulous
pashmina scarf wrapped around you."

GREAT WALL AND
TRIM COMBOS

We all know how to do blue walls with white trim. Now what about some more intriguing color pairings, like eggplant and pale green? Wake up a bedroom or den with one of these inspired combinations.

"Parma Gray is a soft, soothing blue that feels like the ocean. I needed a nice contrast, and came up with chocolate brown—like earth against the sky."

SCOTT SANDERS
FARROW & BALL | PARMA GRAY 27 (TOP)
| MAHOGANY 36 (BOTTOM)

PAOLO MOSCHINO
FARROW & BALL | LIGHT BLUE 22 (TOP)
| OLD WHITE 4 (BOTTOM)
"I never treat a bathroom as a bathroom, but as another room in the house. The first thing I bought was the painting, and the colors came out of it. There's a powdery blue on the walls and a powdery gray on the wainscoting. It's a soothing combination."

JENNIFER GARRIGUES
BENJAMIN MOORE | PALLADIAN BLUE HC-144
| HOLLINGSWORTH GREEN HC-141

"I like washed-out blue walls, surrounded by the most heavenly shade of green for the trim. It reminds me of the changing colors of the ocean on a sunny day, or the sea glass you find when you're strolling on the beach. Add a splash of cobalt and a dash of dusty pink and see what that does for your senses!"

ERIC LYSDAHL
BENJAMIN MOORE | LAKE PLACID 827
| WHIRLPOOL 1436

"This is a classic Gustavian palette, with a wispy blue on the walls and a cloudy blue on the moldings—like glacial water reflected against a late afternoon sky. The colors have a grayish cast, which gives them a built-in patina, so the room never seems to age. It's already faded. There's something sort of calm and happy about that."

ELAINE GRIFFIN
RALPH LAUREN PAINT | CAPRI PINK VM71
| CHOCOLATE SOUFFLÉ VM90

"I'm wild about sophisticated color combos like coral walls with twig-brown trim—or vice versa. It's fresh and unexpected, but actually, the Brits have been doing it for centuries. The rosy pink has character and warmth and really flatters everything in the room—people and furniture. It's like blush for your wall. And the brown ties in with what's happening on the floor and your dark brown furniture."

MALCOLM JAMES KUTNER
PRATT & LAMBERT | SUBTLE ORANGE 9-7
| BLACKWATCH GREEN 19-17

"I recently painted a living room the color of lobster bisque, lacquered to give it the depth to stand up to black trim. Very London 1930s, as if it's eternally cocktail hour and Evelyn Waugh could walk in at any moment. The black trim did it, but I never use pure black. Here it was tinted with green so it's not quite so strident. The room is adventurous, but people still feel secure—and they look good."

WHITNEY STEWART
BENJAMIN MOORE | CAPONATA AF-650
| THICKET AF-405

"Aubergine on the walls conveys a sense of deep space, like a Mark Rothko painting. It's expansive and tonally rich. Then I'd be audacious and mix it with an equally provocative trim color like this citron gray-green. It might be too much for a bedroom or a living room, but try it in a study, a library, or a powder room."

DARREN HENAULT
FARROW & BALL | SAND 45
| DORSET CREAM 68

"In a living room, I painted not only the moldings but the panels in between in Dorset Cream, and then used Sand on the remainder of the walls. Sand is the color of wet sand—a mucky, muddy brown with a little red in it to perk it up. In a big room, you wouldn't necessarily want too much of it, but the Dorset Cream trim sweetens it and keeps the room light and bright."

BASIL WALTER

DONALD KAUFMAN COLOR | DKC-63
| DKC-50

"The reason these colors work so well together is that they're the most natural combination, like the green leaves and brown bark of a tree. I think there's something therapeutic about pale green walls, and the nutty brown trim has an undertone of green. That reflection back and forth adds to the sense of peace. I'd use these in a smaller, more intimate room where you read or listen to music. They let you drift into imaginary worlds even with your eyes wide open."

CAROL GLASSER

PRATT & LAMBERT | ARROWROOT 29-32
| PHANTOM 11-31

"The Swedes were brilliant at using paint to create architectural detail, even where there was none, and we followed their example in a dining room. The walls were painted Arrowroot, a chalky white, and then we outlined them in a slightly darker shade to mimic an 18th-century trim. The colors are pale and dreamy, as if you were seeing them by candlelight."

ALEXANDER DOHERTY
FARROW & BALL | PICTURE GALLERY RED 42
| CHARLESTON GRAY 243

"I like what are referred to as 'dirty' colors," says Alexander Doherty of the New York apartment he painted in an unusual combination of muddied reds, grays, and blues. For the master bedroom, he took his cue from the muted palette of the homeowners' artwork and coated the walls in a creamy rose with a soft gray trim (a favorite shade of Bloomsbury group artists).

CHARLES O. SCHWARZ III
FARROW & BALL | LIGHT BLUE 22
| PIGEON 25

A Scandinavian aesthetic permeates this weekend house decorated by Charles O. Schwarz III. He opted for cool blues and greys for the bootroom, painting the wood without primer so the knots of the pine paneling would show through for character.

CHERYL KATZ

FARROW & BALL | HARDWICK WHITE 5
BENJAMIN MOORE | HEAVEN 2118-70

"In a house by the ocean we painted the kitchen this beautiful, changeable gray that spans the arc from green to gray to blue, depending on the light. Then we chose a pale, pale lavender for the trim. It's rather ethereal and very luminescent, as if it has an inner glow."

WILLIAM R. EUBANKS

SHERWIN-WILLIAMS | HEARTTHROB SW 6866
| TANAGER SW 6601

"For a red-on-red library, I chose a vibrant Chinese red in high gloss and painted the walls about six times, to get real depth. Then I used a slightly browner red on the moldings to create a shadow line and add a little contrast. The combination is bold and intense, but oddly enough it's a very relaxing room. The red just pulls you in."

Benjamin Moore's Super White, already
on the walls of Thomas Jayne's New York
loft, turned out to be the perfect backdrop
for his vibrant color blocks.

QUICK COLOR FIXES

Is there a dark corner of your dining room that you'd like to brighten up? Or do you want to add a little zest to the kitchen? Here are some easy color tricks to add a bit of design flair.

"When I moved into a big white loft, all my furniture looked lost. So I painted these floating cubes of color on the walls to anchor a few pieces, and it had this great effect. Absolutely transporting."

THOMAS JAYNE
BENJAMIN MOORE | SMASHING PINK 1303 (TOP)
| BLUE BELLE 782 (BOTTOM)

Rather than scrap the 1980s maple bookcases in this California living room, designer Jay Jeffers updated them with paint.

JAY JEFFERS
BENJAMIN MOORE | BUXTON BLUE HC-149 (TOP)
| RUST 2175-30 (BOTTOM)
"It's the contrast of cool Wedgewood blue with terra-cotta that makes this bookcase interesting. If I had painted it all blue, it would have disappeared. But now the dark paint on the back wall makes a dramatic backdrop for all the family photos and accessories."

CHRISTOPHER COLEMAN

BENJAMIN MOORE | COOL AQUA 2056-40

"Why not put the color in the closet? Nothing like being a little uncomfortable arriving for dinner, the host takes your coat, opens the closet door, and wow! You get a big dose of turquoise. It gets the conversation going—and distracts from the mess."

SUZANNE KASLER

FARROW & BALL | ORANGERY 70

"Paint one wall and it will change the whole feel of a room. I'd use this vibrant, earthy orange in a dining room, on the wall with the buffet, and bring in more color with decorative items."

MILES REDD

BENJAMIN MOORE | ICY BLUE 2057-70 (TOP)
| HERITAGE RED EXTERIOR ROOM (BOTTOM)

"People never think about doors and ceilings as places for color. Think how chic it would be to have chalky white walls with black, black, trim, a pale blue ceiling, and lipstick red doors—in high gloss. Blue and red look so regal. It would make eveyone feel like the Duke of Windsor."

LARRY LASLO

BENJAMIN MOORE | LADYBUG RED 1322

"I love to see a painted staircase—not the tread itself, but the vertical part. Most people leave it white, but it always gets kicked up. So make it barn red—just flat, clear, clean color."

ALESSANDRA BRANCA

DONALD KAUFMAN COLOR COLLECTION | DKC-23

"Update a plain white kitchen with apple green stripes—vertical, definitely. Ten inches wide if the ceiling is eight feet high or less."

TOM STRINGER

RALPH LAUREN PAINT | PRUSSIAN BLUE VM122

"Paint the interior of the lampshades. Then you have these white card stock shades with a little peek of color—like this beautiful, watercolory Easter egg shade of blue."

BIRCH COFFEY

BENJAMIN MOORE | CARBON COPY 2117-10

"I stole this from a friend born in Baltimore, where at some point it became very fashionable to paint your baseboards black. Just the flat part, not the upper molding. Instantly you get this crisp graphic element, as if you've underlined the room."

**BENJAMIN MOORE
SUMMER BLUE 2067-50**
A well-placed jolt of color can have a surprising impact on a room. Choose this richly saturated blue to set off the softer blues in the ceiling wallpaper.

WHITNEY STEWART

C2 | CAFÉ LATTE 7314 (TOP)
| CHAI 7293 (BOTTOM)

"Make your own virtual moldings. Do circles within squares or simple rectangles. I like this warm, pretty brown against a straw color. Get out an inch-wide brush and just start painting. If it's all perfectly taped out, it loses its charm."

Sometimes the best place for color isn't on the wall. Color consultant Eve Ashcraft used a muted peridot paint on the floorboards, injecting a splash of gemlike color into an all-white bathroom. Using durable oil gloss enamel ensures a hard-wearing finish.

GIL SCHAFER AND EVE ASHCRAFT
PRATT & LAMBERT | PERIDOT 18-20

DD ALLEN

MODERN MASTERS | VENETIAN BLUE ME-429

"Don't forget the floor—it's such an underutilized opportunity for color. In a downtown loft, we were going for a Moroccan feeling, with limed white walls and a Mediterranean blue floor for a wonderful cool, watery feeling. It's a metallic paint, so it really sparkles."

KELLY WEARSTLER

PRATT & LAMBERT | SCARLET O'HARA 1870

"Color on the ceiling is very tempting, like dipping your toe in the pool. I would use a really beautiful red. Some are too purple but this has more orange, which I think is a little sexier. It definately makes a space feel more intimate and gives some energy."

The ceiling was glazed in a custom off-white
with a touch of gold to pick up on the glint of
all the acting awards.

FRONT DOORS WITH STYLE

A freshly painted entrance is the easiest of makeovers, adding instant curb appeal. Why not pick pumpkin or plum or shocking pink and make an unforgettable first impression?

"This is a house in the California chaparral, at the foot of a California mountain range. The land is covered with mesquite and mustard weed. This color evokes the notion of shade, beckoning the visitor inside, hinting at the cool to be found within."

KATHRYN M. IRELAND
FARROW & BALL | FOLLY GREEN 76

CARL D'AQUINO

BENJAMIN MOORE | MOUNTAIN RIDGE 1456
| CHIC LIME 396

"Go with something strong and bold that makes a statement. I like this gorgeous raisin with undertones of purple and gray and brown. It's an unusual color for a front door. A little mysterious. It would whet the palate for the entry foyer. Why not do that in something exciting and complementary, like Chic Lime?"

MATTHEW PATRICK SMYTH

PRATT & LAMBERT | BEESWAX 11-6

"This would be a great color to come home to at the end of a hard day. It reminds me of Provence and those van Gogh fields full of harvested wheat. It's got that baked-in-the-sun look. I like it because it's warm, but not one of those shock-value yellows. Unexpected, but not out of the ballpark. It's one of those colors that just has a glow."

GARY MCBOURNIE
BENJAMIN MOORE | SAILOR'S SEA BLUE 2063-40
"The blue on this boathouse door is one I use constantly. It's softer and warmer than a hard, sharp blue, and it just feels like Nantucket, where you're in the middle of the ocean and there's blue all around you. It makes me think of sunshine on water and sailboats and mermaids and good times at the beach."

SUZANNE TUCKER
FINE PAINTS OF EUROPE |
TULIP RED 1001
"I wanted to draw people to the door like bees to a flower, and this luscious red did the trick. The color has such clarity. It's like the most kissable lips."

PHILIP GORRIVAN

BENJAMIN MOORE | HAMPSHIRE ROCKS 1450

"Grays can be so dull, but this has a little kick to it. It's such a sophisticated shade of gray, with that lavender cast. It reminds me of the gray one sees in Georgian interiors, particularly the Adam houses in the English countryside. In high gloss, pure elegance!"

ANGIE HRANOWSKY

BENJAMIN MOORE | VENEZUELAN SEA 2054-30

"This is a deep, dark blue-green, almost like a jewel tone or something you'd see on a peacock feather. It's fun to experiment with your front door. You don't have to go crazy with the whole house, and you could do it in an afternoon. Add a pair of plants—in beautiful pots, of course."

KEN FULK

C2 | WICKED 6446

"When you first see this deep, rich purple, it looks quite dark, but there's a good dose of red plum underneath. It would look kind of dapper on a door, very Savile Row. Dark and distinguished, yet unexpected. And it would work equally well on a traditional or a modern house."

STEPHEN SHUBEL

BENJAMIN MOORE | SUNBURST 2023-40

"Shingle Style house with white trim and a bright lemon yellow door would be very welcoming, and a little daring. In summer, it would look great with greenery and flowers, and in winter, it would brighten up that barren feeling."

PHOEBE HOWARD

FARROW & BALL | CARRIAGE GREEN 94

"Dark green is a traditional Southern color that looks wonderful on the front doors of brick houses with white trim. This green is so dark it's almost black, but when the sun hits it you clearly see the green. It's the color of a spruce tree. I'd do it in high gloss, super thick, like those beautiful Georgian front doors you see in England with a round brass doorknob right in the center."

WHITNEY STEWART

BENJAMIN MOORE | GOLD RUSH 2166-10 (TOP)
                | OLIVE BRANCH 2143-30 (BOTTOM)

"I would use this pumpkin with olive trim. It's a bold color that pushes the envelope for a front door. It says, 'I dare you to walk through.' But then it's also very appealing. It's the new paradigm for anyone who is tired of red doors. It's more youthful."

ANNIE SELKE
BENJAMIN MOORE | DROP DEAD GORGEOUS 1329
When designer Annie Selke renovated her 1960s ranch house, she chose a lipstick pink front door. "It just needed something," she says. "The exterior was so calm and restrained everywhere else. I can change it out—it's easy to repaint—but I like what it says, that I'm willing to be a little playful. You can see it for miles."

ANDREW FLESHER
BENJAMIN MOORE | EVENING SKY 833

"This is a deep, dark inky blue that can look almost black in the shade, but it turns into a rich, deep blue in the sun. It would look just as great on a stone house in the mountains as it would on a faded, silvery-shingled Cape Cod at the beach."

In the 1960s, **D**avid Hicks designed his **C**helsea apartment and lacquered the walls of his living room in a color he called "**C**oca-Cola."

COLOR WE'VE BEEN DYING TO TRY

What colors do designers really, *really* want to use, but haven't had the chance yet? They're just waiting for the right room.

"This room, lacquered a "Coca-Cola" color, sealed it—David Hicks was the James Bond of interior design. Wow! It's a great bold sexy statement. I would do it in this very dark brown, in a full gloss finish as he did, so it becomes luminous."

PETER DUNHAM
FARROW & BALL | MAHOGANY 36

BOBBY MCALPINE

RALPH LAUREN PAINT | WALTON CREAM VM65 (TOP)
| LINEN UL03 (BOTTOM)

"I'm aching to do pink. This particular shade is
sort of an apparition, like something that used to
be pink and this is all that's left of it. Very, very
tender. I'd pair it with a nice stone color that
would kindly allow the pink to step one little foot
forward. For the fabrics, just change the texture —
cashmere, powdery silk, nubby wool. Be
enveloped by it."

STEPHEN SHUBEL

KELLY-MOORE | CACTUS CAFÉ KM3431-3

"There's a café in Paris that has this unusual green
on the walls, a kind of old-world color that makes
you feel relaxed and calm. Think of a mossy
garden after the rain."

BRETT BELDOCK

BENJAMIN MOORE | GRAPPA 1393

"My dear departed Ron Grimaldi was the most
elegant man, totally over the top, and he
painted everything eggplant. It looked deep and
mysterious and kind of sexy. I see it with silver,
light blue, green, orange. I'd treat it as a neutral
so I wouldn't be afraid of it."

MARY McDONALD

BENJAMIN MOORE | CORAL PINK 2003-50

"I have a huge drawer for any color I come across that I like. Right now it contains a pink napkin from the Beverly Hills Hotel, a shard from a broken green vase, tear sheets from magazines, some chocolate-covered coffee beans, and red and soft pink boxes from a Paris pastry shop. I had to buy pastries in order to get the boxes."

MARY DOUGLAS DRYSDALE

BEHR | YAM 290B-7

"I love the warmth and inferred light that comes from lively, zesty, orangey colors. Since this has a little brown in it, it doesn't have the brass that orange does. It's more sophisticated, dressier. Often a valuable rug or a rare antique carries a room, but in this case it's the paint that would be dazzling."

DAN BARSANTI

BENJAMIN MOORE | ALLIGATOR ALLEY 441

"In *The War of the Roses*, Danny DeVito's office was the hottest-looking thing I've ever seen. Every nook and cranny was painted this great loden green, with a bit of yellow in it, which makes it look more hip than hunter green. It's a classic luxe look—a great backdrop for books, art, mahogany furniture."

RODERICK SHADE

BENJAMIN MOORE | PINK CORSAGE 1349

"I bought a vintage *Superfly* movie poster in this fuschia. Then I saw kind of '60s cut velvet by Osborne & Little in fuchsia and taupe and thought this was the start of a color scheme. Fuchsia is rockin'. I like the way it pairs with strong neutrals like taupe and wenge brown."

ANGIE HRANOWSKY
BENJAMIN MOORE
WHITE CHOCOLATE OC-127

"Don't get me wrong, I love white, but I love it for contrast. I see an all-white room and I think oh, man, that's great, but if you'd throw some fuchsia pillows on that sofa . . . I kept this bedroom mostly neutral, adding pops of color for a romantic, feminine quality."

WHITNEY STEWART

C2 | ENOKI 425

"I'm always looking for the new neutral. This is it, a soft camel that has red and green and yellow in it. That's why it goes with everything. Can't you just imagine it with icy blues? Chutney orange and sage? Or black and white—always smart. When a color transcends itself to coordinate with so many different colors and still retains warmth, it jumps to that ethereal level. It's a color you just love to be around. You would feel like a million dollars in a room painted this color."

MARK EPSTEIN

BENJAMIN MOORE | DEEP RIVER 1582

"Paint a room this warm charcoal gray, with dove white trim, and you'd get an instant sense of architecture. It has all the warmth and coziness of a paneled room and the fantastic, moody, earthy stonelike walls convey a sense of drama."

FRANK ROOP

C2 | EXPEDITION 162

"An intense olive brown with undernotes of chartreuse. It would look amazing in matte on the walls and high gloss on the ceiling."

ERINN VALENCICH

DUNN-EDWARDS | DEEP CARNATION DE5011

"David Weidman did these really cool color-block prints in the '70s. The one I have is reds layered with purples and this intense deep violet pink. I see it with a funky mustardy green or turquoise."

RICHARD MISHAAN

BENJAMIN MOORE | CHILI PEPPER 2004-20

"This is a really deep coral, kind of like a cheerful Chinese red. Pinks and reds to me are synonymous with frozen drinks and relaxing."

OPPOSITE PAGE:

The buttery yellow on the walls of this preteen boy's room contrasts sharply with the white ribs of the overhang, creating the effect of a ship's berth.

JODI MACKLIN

DONALD KAUFMAN COLOR COLLECTION | DKC-20

Dark brown plays up the gleaming lines
of modern furniture. And bright green
leaves pop.

COLORS **MEN LOVE**

He may be bold at work and at play, but when it comes to picking colors for his home, he plays it safe. Here are some colors that will encourage a guy to take some chances.

"This dark, warm, rich bronze is very, very sexy. Strong and masculine, yet it doesn't shout. It can take any room from casual to sophisticated. It works really well with metal furniture. I've put purple and lavender, yellow and orange up against it, and they really set each other off."

PHILIP NIMMO
BENJAMIN MOORE | NORTH CREEK BROWN 1001

MARY McDONALD
RALPH LAUREN | YELLOWHAMMER GH100
"Men are open to a soft yellow. When their wives are trying to do something too pastelly, they'll say, 'How about yellow? I can deal with yellow.' It's classic, neutral, safe. I can't tell you how many yellow living rooms I've done. This is a wonderful butter yellow, a little dirty, which takes the girly part out of it."

MARTYN LAWRENCE-BULLARD
FARROW & BALL | RADICCHIO 96

"My current favorite, I confess, is burgundy. For years it was considered outmoded, but now it looks fresh again. Try lacquering the walls of a study in Farrow & Ball's classic burgundy, and contrast it with ivory-painted bookcases and creamy glove-leather club chairs. So chic. Throw in a Paul Evans table or two and you just became the hippest man-about-town."

MARIO BUATTA
BENJAMIN MOORE | GREAT BARRINGTON GREEN HC-122

"Most men are clueless about color. If I ask a man, 'What color is your bedroom?' he says, 'I have to ask my wife.' They stick with safe colors. But they do like this green. It's a yellowy olive green, more contemporary than dark hunter green. I see it in a library with white woodwork."

JAMIE DRAKE
BENJAMIN MOORE | ARUBA BLUE 2048-30

"We painted a library a vibrant shade of turquoisey green—a modern twist on a classic tradition. And then we did all the woodwork in high-gloss black. Very chic, yet totally masculine—like a two-tone Bugatti from the 1920s."

THOMAS JAYNE

BENJAMIN MOORE | CAMEL BACK 1103

"It's just an extremely flattering color, and camel-colored walls are warm and soft, yet very masculine. Camel, with an underpinning of yellow and a slight bit of red, has much more life than beige, which can go gray and cold. Art looks great on it."

MILES REDD

FINE PAINTS OF EUROPE | COLONIAL ROSE 7102T

"I had a client, a very elegant man in his seventies, who requested a pink bedroom. He was a widower, and it reminded him of his wife. I think men like pink more than they're willing to admit. Men tend to like warm colors. This pink has a happy carnation quality in bright sunlight and gets more glowy and dusty at night."

PETER DUNHAM

BENJAMIN MOORE | CITRUS BLAST 2018-30 (TOP)

| MYSTICAL GRAPE 2071-30 (BOTTOM)

"If you're trying to sell a guy on color, just pick the colors of his favorite sports team. The Lakers' colors are the choice of every man in L.A. I have even done the felt on a pool table. I think I should do a line of fabrics—stripes—based on the colors of famous teams."

PAULA PERLINI
BENJAMIN MOORE | MOROCCAN RED 1309
In this library designed by Paula Perlini, the high wainscot, painted a cool white, is a crisp conterpart to the eye-catching strip of red.

The soft chai color designer Stephen Brady chose for this bedroom lends a depth and Old World sophistication to the walls. The warmth and matte velvet texture of the paint anchor the overall palette and serves to beautifully highlight the British Colonial feel of the furnishings.

STEPHEN BRADY

SHERWIN-WILLIAMS | BAGEL 6114

PHOEBE HOWARD

BENJAMIN MOORE | SOFT PUMPKIN 2166-40

"I was doing a high-rise beach condo in Florida in greens and blues and sandy colors, and the husband kept trying to throw in some orange. I said, 'No, no, no. I'm only using colors you can see around here.' So he invited me over for cocktails one night and took me to the window when the sun was setting. 'See? What about that?'"

CLODAGH

BENJAMIN MOORE | MIDNIGHT NAVY 2067-10

"Ask any man what his favorite color is, and he'll probably say blue. It's a thoughtful color. There's a mystery to deep, deep indigo blue. Beautiful in a bedroom—it helps promote sleep. I love it with golds and burnished metallics. It's limitless."

KEITH IRVINE

BENJAMIN MOORE | CORAL GABLES 2010-40

"I've done a lot of rooms for men in paneled
wood and leather. Then I'll highlight the back
of a bookcase with a bit of lively coral. Men like
that color because it reminds them of something
to drink. Add an animal print—Stark's Ocelot
carpet. Supermasculine and comfortable."

CHAPTER

3

INSPIRATION
FROM AROUND
THE WORLD

Black and white and green is eye-catching, and in this study
Minster Green becomes a strong, unexpected backdrop to a collection
of photography.

COLORS FROM YOUR TRAVELS

Visiting a new place gives us unforgettable influences: the fiery red of a Masai *shúkà*; Greece's brilliant cerulean blue island rooftops; the dark smoky taupe of the Caspian Sea.

"I was on safari in South Africa at the Royal Malewane, the most extraordinary private game reserve. When a dazzle of zebras ran in front of our jeep, it took my breath away to see those stripes framed against the bush."

MARTYN LAWRENCE-BULLARD
FARROW & BALL | MINSTER GREEN 224

JEFFREY BILHUBER

FINE PAINTS OF EUROPE | 2030-G70Y

"I've been spending more time in Santa Barbara, up in the hills where you see a particular yellow-based green. It's kind of a cross-pollination of sage and olive and eucalyptus and palm. Not a grass green but a salty green, as if it has a hint of the ocean."

"The hint of lilac in my mother's Oushak rug inspired the wall color in the living room. Then I pulled fuchsia, raspberry, and orange accents from the painting on the mantel and mixed them with golden yellow. The colors absolutely sing in that room."

ANGIE HRANOWSKY
PORTER PAINTS | PERSIAN PINK 6650-1

SUZANNE RHEINSTEIN
RALPH LAUREN PAINT | BLUE-GREEN GH81

"Lago Argentino is a glacier lake in Patagonia, and it's the most amazing color, an aqua, milky because as the ice melts it pulls minerals off the mountain. I stayed in an inn with a stunning view of the Perito Moreno glacier."

PETER DUNHAM
BENJAMIN MOORE | BLUE ANGEL 2058-70

"I was in Oranienbaum in Russia, wandering through this tumbledown park, and suddenly there was this pavilion that looked like a delicately iced wedding cake, painted the blue of a Baltic summer sky. So romantic, and it turns out to have been the takeoff point for an 18th-century royal roller coaster."

ELISSA CULLMAN

BENJAMIN MOORE | DALILA 319

"One of my favorite spots in Florence is sitting on the balcony of the Lungarno Hotel—all those shades of sun drenched yellow. It's a color you see in every Italian town; you wonder how they got it so right."

KATHRYN M. IRELAND

RALPH LAUREN PAINT | GOLDFINCH GH105

"Lecce, Italy, is famous for its Baroque architecture—it's that plaster that looks good only after 400 years. And it changes in different lights—apricot one minute and almost burnt siena the next."

SUSAN ZISES GREEN

FARROW & BALL | MENAGERIE 63

"We were driving in the countryside outside of Delhi and saw all these women out in the fields in their exquisite saris, in every shade from yellow to gold to this luscious melony terra-cotta."

SARA BENGUR

FARROW & BALL | BLUE GROUND 210

"I always visit the harem at the Topkapi Palace, Istanbul, where the sultan lived with hundreds of women. You see this vivid turquoise on the 16th-century tiles along the walls."

ALEX PAPACHRISTIDIS

BENJAMIN MOORE | OPAL ESSENCE 680

"Ever since I was a teenager, we've been going to the Hotel du Cap on the French Riviera and staying at Eden Roc, right on the water with the waves crashing against the rocks. The Mediterranean is deep aqua and I wanted to re-create that feeling, but in a lighter version for a bedroom's walls—a kind of sea foamy aqua."

Walking through this guest bedroom makes you feel as if you are wading through the lakes of color consultant Eve Ashcraft's Michigan childhood.

GIL SCHAFER AND EVE ASHCRAFT
PRATT & LAMBERT
| FRESH CREAM 11-5 (TOP)
| WINDSOR BLUE 27-19 (BOTTOM)

Raspberry with cream: In this octagonal
anteroom between master bedroom and
bath, Gary McBournie added a dollop of
Benjamin Moore's White Dove on the trim.

BRIGHT SUMMER DAYS

What is the palette of summer? Is it the soft pink of cherry Italian ice or the icy green of crushed mint leaves at the bottom of a mojito? Explore the colors of summer and make them your own.

"I like the warmth and cheeriness of this really deep raspberry, almost the color of a pink Corvette. It has that nice old Florida look, before everyone went beige. You need an intense color down here to absorb the light."

GARY MCBOURNIE
BENJAMIN MOORE | FLORIDA PINK 1320

OPPOSITE PAGE:

Aqua and pale blues are always evocative of the ocean. In the upstairs hallway of this Long Island beach house, designer Ruthie Sommers chose a color that feels very much like the color of water in the shallows of the Caribbean. An added decorative element—an apothecary jar filled with seashells—summons up memories of tranquil hours at the beach.

RUTHIE SOMMERS

BENJAMIN MOORE | SEA FOAM 2123-60

CARL D'AQUINO

BENJAMIN MOORE | POTPOURRI GREEN 2029-50

"I'm just back from Milan, where I ate gelato twice a day. Such amazing colors! Pistachio is my favorite, but I don't want to gain weight so I'll just surround myself with this creamy green, instead of eating it."

JARRETT HEDBORG

BENJAMIN MOORE | SANTA MONICA BLUE 776

"This deep indigo blue is a classic beach house color. After three hours of sitting in traffic on an August afternoon, you want to collapse in a room that will complement an ice-cold martini."

TIMOTHY WHEALON

RALPH LAUREN PAINT | BASALT VM121

"It feels like fresh air when you walk into the room. And it does read as blue—the palest, softest blue, as if you were floating in the sky. Very ethereal and dreamy."

JACKIE TERRELL

BENJAMIN MOORE | LEMON FREEZE 2025-50

"This is an acidy yellow green, kind of hip and very sunny, but not in a cornball way. More exotic, like a color you'd see on a tropical island."

CELERIE KEMBLE

ROLLINSON HUES | 31

"Christopher Rollinson's paints have such saturation and depth. This warm, luminous green feels as fresh and summer sweet as a box of sugar snap peas and captures the very essence of a farmer's market."

LEE MELAHN

BENJAMIN MOORE | PERSIAN VIOLET 1419

"We pulled this lavender from the evening sky and summer flowers like lilac and lupine. In the bright sun, it takes on a warmth that brings out the red in the purple, but then as the light fades, it cools down and becomes this beautiful blue."

JENNIFER GARRIGUES
PORTER PAINTS |
PARSLEY TINT 6998-1
This pale aqua green is like the ocean when it's so clear you can see the sand through the water. It reminds me of holidays and sunshine and how calm you feel when you sit on the shore and watch the waves breaking.

In this Florida bedroom by Jennifer Garrigues, sea green walls are set off by a Benjamin Moore white on the trim.

MYRA HOEFER
BENJAMIN MOORE | QUEEN ANNE PINK HC-60
The pink walls of this bedroom remind designer **Myra Hoefer** of a worn and beloved pair of ballet slippers: silky, soft, and subtle. The color brings this antique red lacquer desk to life.

FRANK ROOP

BENJAMIN MOORE | SOFT FERN 2144-40

"For me, the most appealing colors in summer are not hot but cool. You don't need to be reminded of the sun and heat—you're in it. What you want is a cool breeze through the pine trees, like this chalky gray green."

MIMI MCMAKIN

SHERWIN-WILLIAMS | IN THE PINK SW 6583

"Here in Florida, I have the most wonderful porch that has been painted pink for 30 years. It's the pink of strawberry ice cream cones and climbing roses and the blush on our cheeks after a long, luxurious day at the beach."

MAUREEN FOOTER

BENJAMIN MOORE | OLD WORLD 2011-40

"Imagine walking right into a peony. This color is on the cusp between pink and coral, with a yellow undertone that makes it more sophisticated and versatile than a pinky pink. If only it could smell like a flower!"

The ottoman is covered in Mayfair stripe in plum by
Randolph & Hein. The cast-resin floor lamp is by
Oly Studio.

FOR A SUNNY ROOM

Should you go bright to stand up to the sun or soft and cool to subdue it? Designers share their brilliant strategies for using color to capture and tame sunlight.

"This is an elegant yacht, and here is a beautiful custom 1930s-style bed upholstered in white piqué and nailhead trim, looking out of a large porthole. And the view, oh my gosh! This is not your classic blue and white room. It's sweet and understated."

MYRA HOEFER
BENJAMIN MOORE | MISTY MEMORIES 2118-60

EUGENIE NIVEN

BENJAMIN MOORE | SEAFOAM GREEN 2039-60

"It's a cool, minty green, like those striped cabañas on the beach in St. Tropez in the 1940s. I would never paint a really sunny room yellow. You'd feel like you were sitting on the surface of the sun."

JACKYE LANHAM

SHERWIN-WILLIAMS | MAGNETIC GRAY SW-7058

"In the South, sunny means hot. We don't want colors that make you turn the air-conditioning up. This is a silvery blue-gray, almost like an Armani color, very soothing. Because of the grayness, it absorbs light."

DIANE CHAPMAN

BENJAMIN MOORE | TANGERINE FUSION 083

"Something like chrome yellow or shocking pink would be too intense. But this color is just divine. It reminds me of walking into a frothy orangeade or floating on a scoop of orange sherbet."

DAN CARITHERS

BENJAMIN MOORE | FERNWOOD GREEN 2145-40

"This is a green that has a slight haze to it, like early-morning dew on a lawn. You know it's green, but it doesn't reek of it. At different times of the day, it changes color, but it's always still with you."

RUBY BEETS
BENJAMIN MOORE | SMOKE EMBERS 1466
This subtle gray chosen by designer Ruby Beets provides a
quiet contrast to the stark white of the ceiling and trim. It
also uses the sunlight to elegantly highlight the texture of
the plank walls in the living room.

In Nancy Braithwaite's Atlanta bedroom, moldings and baseboards in Pratt & Lambert's Pearly Gates 2268 provide a graphic contrast to dark walls.

NANCY BRAITHWAITE
BENJAMIN MOORE | VAN BUREN BROWN HC-70
"When you go out into the sun, the first thing you do is put on sunglasses. You want to tamp down the glare, so your eyes don't squint. This is a deep tobacco brown that will give a room a certain sense of depth and character, even if it has absolutely no architectural interest."

JOSIE MCCARTHY

SHERWIN-WILLIAMS | IVOIRE SW6127

"This is a scrumptious color that reminds me of my favorite patisserie in Paris, where they have this wonderful yellow cake with raspberry sauce."

MARTYN LAWRENCE-BULLARD

FARROW & BALL | BLUE GROUND 210

"There is nothing more uplifting than a room not only drenched in sunshine but also in color. I love the way this turquoise makes me feel, especially when the sun hits it."

MICHAEL BERMAN

DUNN-EDWARDS | PERFECT PEAR DE5519

"It's an absolutely amazing color—pear green with a bit of apple. It goes from being pale in the early morning to something that's bright and pungent in the late afternoon."

JACKIE TERRELL

PRATT & LAMBERT | NASTURTIUM 1830 (TOP)
| GLOAMING 2145 (BOTTOM)

"If I feel like basking in the sun, I'd choose a saffron—very Indian and exotic-looking. But if I want to cut the brightness, I'd choose a dark, foresty brown."

GIL SCHAFER AND EVE ASHCRAFT
PRATT & LAMBERT | GUNNEL 25-23
Gil Schafer chose a smoky gray-blue paint for the floor.
It centers the room, absorbing the brightness of the walls
and windows while at the same time reflecting back a
warmth that adds a much-needed balance.

MALCOLM KUTNER

DONALD KAUFMAN COLOR COLLECTION | DKC-28

"This is the color of light—sort of like crème fraîche and butter and sunlight and moonlight all mixed together. When it's sunshiny, it becomes more creamy, but when it's dark outside, it looks very bright and luminous."

MYRA HOEFER

FARROW & BALL | BONE 15

"You want something that kind of cools it down. This is the color of lichen on a tree, a gray-green that changes with the light. It's calming."

GARY MCBOURNIE

BENJAMIN MOORE | DAVENPORT TAN HC-76

"If a room is too bright, it gets all blown out and you stop seeing things. You want a color that absorbs light, like this dark, smoky brown. It makes me think of cigars and old sepia photographs."

BROOKE HUTTIG

SHERWIN-WILLIAMS | SHAGREEN SW6422

"My loggia faces south, so it's solid sun with white tile floors and a white-beamed ceiling. I glazed the walls with a sea-foamy green to counteract the heat and add a hint of water. Now it feels serene."

SMALL ROOMS

Conventional wisdom says, "Paint it white." But who wants to be conventional? There's a world of gorgeous options—from butter yellow to marine blue—that can give even the tiniest space a big personality.

"If it's already small and dark, make it darker! Then it feels deliberately intimate. This TV room is done in the deepest, darkest chocolate— 85 percent cacao. It feels like the room where the cool kids would hang out."

ERINN VALENCICH
VALSPAR | LABRADOR 3009-9

W. TYSON BURKS

BENJAMIN MOORE | DARK TEAL 2053-20

"A traditional house needed to be more young, like its occupants, so we loosened up the paneled walls in a study with a teal blue. When you're working, you want to be energized, not drained, and color is stimulating. Several coats of gloss gave it a lacquered look."

THOMAS JAYNE

FARROW & BALL | LICHEN 19

"I like a darker color because it creates shadows in the corners. This smoky green would give a small room an air of mystery. It's changeable, looking different in different lights. I see it with warm blues and pinks and crimson. Actually, almost any color will go with green."

NANCY BOSZARDT

C2 | CORNBREAD C2-138

"In a small space, the color of the walls becomes even more important because you can't fit in a lot of furniture. I had a yellow bedroom when I was a child, and every morning I woke up happy. Yellow can be hard to get right, but this feels warm and inviting, like a buttered corn muffin."

MILES REDD

FINE PAINTS OF EUROPE | BAMBOO LEAF 103A

"In a small space I like to take one strong color and use it everywhere. There's something refreshing about emerald green. It puts a modern spin on a tiny Manhattan kitchen and feels cool and sparkling, especially in this glassy finish. Kind of like a gin and tonic."

JEANNETTE WHITSON
FARROW & BALL | HAGUE BLUE 30
"Because this library is small, it lent itself to a rich jewel-box treatment," says designer Jeannette Whitson. She painted the woodwork a deep saturated sapphire and upholstered the u-shaped sofa in a silk velvet very close to the color of the walls.

REBECCA TIER SOSKIN

VALSPAR | APRICOT ICE 2001-2C

"I tend to lean toward lighter tones in a small space, so it doesn't cave in. This has a freshness that feels open and breathable. I see it in a small, enclosed porch with hand-blocked linen in white, blue, and lavender. The sun is setting, and it's time to curl up with a glass of white wine and a good book. I want to be there now!"

LINDSEY BOND

PRATT & LAMBERT | DIPLOMAT GRAY 33-21

"This is not your basic, mousy gray. It has tones of brown and olive that make it more interesting. Paint the walls and trim in a matte finish for an old-world look. Or do it in high gloss for a more contemporary elegance. Either way, it looks great with antiques and art and metallic accents."

CARRIE FUNDINGSLAND

BENJAMIN MOORE | BLACK RASPBERRY 2072-20

"I'm doing a dining room in this deep purple that's almost black—think of a blackberry. Then gray velvet on the chairs, pale avocado linen curtains, a mirrored buffet, a crystal chandelier. Elegance and drama!"

MARIO BUATTA

BENJAMIN MOORE | NEWBURYPORT BLUE HC-155

"I always use a dark color in a small room because it makes it look bigger. And the bigger the furniture, the better. This reminds me of the sea at night, when the moon is rising. It would look very pretty in a bedroom with silver tea paper on the ceiling, to raise the height a bit. Add lavender, pink, turquoise, and white."

KYLE SCHUNEMAN

BENJAMIN MOORE | FLORIDA KEYS BLUE 2050-40

"I dare you to walk into a space painted this color and not smile. It reminds me of that ocean blue you'd see in Belize. My clients were nervous when we started painting, but once it was on all four walls, it had an enveloping effect—cool and soothing. I'd let the walls be the show, and do the furnishings in cream-colored linen, accented with coral."

PETER DUNHAM

OLD FASHIONED MILK PAINT CO. | TAVERN GREEN

"In a small room, you can make a big statement that would be over-the-top in a larger space. This vibrant green is like something you'd see in an Indian miniature. And milk paint has this irregular, chalky quality that feels almost soft, so it's easy to live with. Add peacock blue and black to pump it up, or pink and white if you want to be more feminine."

LILLY BUNN

FINE PAINTS OF EUROPE | VREELAND MINT 3048

"This is as light and refreshing as a scoop of pistachio ice cream—cool and creamy with a little bite to it. Imagine it with an ebonized Jansen chest, a rock-crystal lamp, and a zebra rug. The shine in the enamel paint just adds to the glamour."

BILL BROCKSCHMIDT
BENJAMIN MOORE | MUSTARD OLIVE 2051-10
"This mustard green seemed like a good color for a tall room," says designer Bill Brockschmidt of his 640-square foot apartment. "It's a great backdrop for art, it's a color that works in winter and summer, and it's not so refined that it's off-putting. When the sun comes up and we open the venetian blinds, it's a very relaxing color to live with. At night it glows in candlelight."

FROM THE GARDEN

Fruits, flowers, and foliage: from the deep indigo of eggplant to a morning glory's brilliant azure, nature is filled with lush colors. Borrow some of them for your own palette!

"This dining room has a very different feel; it's modern but with a bit of an ethnic mood. I want an almost sultry feeling. I pulled this deep plum color from this wonderfully rich David Hicks fabric."

ANGIE HRANOWKSY
PRATT & LAMBERT | JACK HORNER'S PLUM 1-20

"I wanted that milky gray-green you see on lamb's ears, with an undertone of silver as the light hits it. Even in winter, it keeps that ethereal, dreamy feeling. One day, I'm going to find a place for the pink."

JAMES SWAN
PRATT & LAMBERT | PEARL WHITE 29-29 (TOP)
| ROSA LEE 1-13 (BOTTOM)

RANDALL BEALE
BENJAMIN MOORE | PEONY 2079-30

"Why not paint a powder room in the hot pink of a Gerber daisy? There's nothing more chic than hot pink walls with white marble floors."

MICHAEL WHALEY
BENJAMIN MOORE | CEDAR GROVE 444

"In my cutting garden I have morning glories climbing over a lattice obelisk painted this wonderful silvery sage green. It reminds me of lavender leaves."

KENNETH BROWN
BENJAMIN MOORE | STRAW 2154-50

"If you look into a calla lily, you'll see those little pollen stems in exactly this color—a golden yellow with a little apricot and peach to take off the edge."

In a Boston living room, designer James Swan
matched the color on the walls to the pale gray-green
of lamb's ears and painted the trim **Pratt & Lambert
POR2343 FB**.

DAN CARITHERS

BENJAMIN MOORE | BRAZILIAN BLUE 817

"Plumbago has tiny flowers, like phlox, and they're purplish blue, which has a cooling effect in a garden as well as a room. It's the prettiest color, so intense. An intense color can still be soft as long as it has a few shadows in it. This is a peaceful, late-evening blue."

ANN DUPUY

FARROW & BALL | PINK GROUND 202

"This is a very serene pink, the color of an old French rose called Cuisse de Nymphe, which translates as the thigh of a nymph. So charming. And everybody looks good against pink."

PATRICIA HEALING

BENJAMIN MOORE | FRENCH LILAC 1403

"My wisteria went absolutely crazy and gave me a whole new way of looking at lavender. Use this pale lilac with brown and white fabric, or navy blue. Very sophisticated."

S. RUSSELL GROVES

PRATT & LAMBERT | MOSS GREEN 16-29

"This is a great mossy green, very soft because of all the gray in it. There's nothing softer on bare feet than a carpet of moss. It feels like kitten fur."

KENDALL WILKINSON
BENJAMIN MOORE
　| LINEN WHITE 70 (LEFT)
　| JET STREAM 814 (RIGHT)
This is a cool shade that wavers between blue and lavender, a color you see in delphinium and hyacinth. It reads as blue on the wall, but the lilac undertones warm it up and make it more soothing.

On a sunny day, the walls are almost robin's egg blue. In the fog it turns a soft blue-gray.

AMY LAU

BENJAMIN MOORE | RUMBA ORANGE 2014-20

"It looks just like those dancing orange nasturtiums that climb and spill and ramble all over the garden. But I'd only use it in a low dose, as an accent color behind a bed or on a wall in a beach house, à la Barragán. Otherwise it would be overpowering."

WARM SHADES

A little of these colors goes a long way, so use them as accents and not on walls. Paint window frames, a door, a piece of furniture from the flea market, maybe even a bed frame—your room will come alive.

The surest way to freshen up a room is to borrow color straight from nature's infinite palette. With a bouquet of possibilities, the only difficult part comes in narrowing down the field. How can we pick just one?

Orange Lily
GLIDDEN
DESERT ORANGE
78YR39/593

Yellow Ranunculus
PRATT & LAMBERT
CANARY YELLOW 12-8

Red Rose
GLIDDEN
DRUM BEAT 00YR08/409

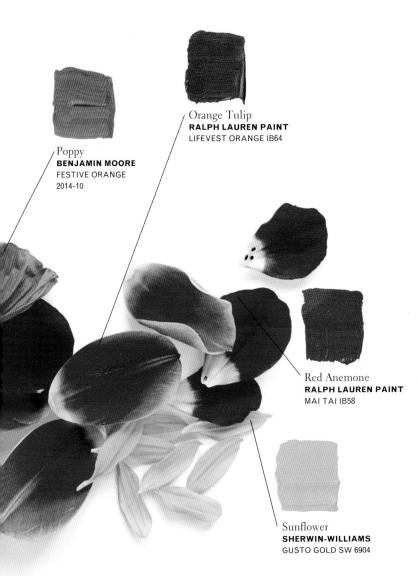

Poppy
BENJAMIN MOORE
FESTIVE ORANGE
2014-10

Orange Tulip
RALPH LAUREN PAINT
LIFEVEST ORANGE IB64

Red Anemone
RALPH LAUREN PAINT
MAI TAI IB58

Sunflower
SHERWIN-WILLIAMS
GUSTO GOLD SW 6904

COOL SHADES

A word about finishes. Light colors look darker in a flat finish. Dark colors look brighter in a gloss or semigloss. A flat finish will work well for the lighter shades here, but the deep purples and pinks will definitely look better with a sheen.

Hyacinth
PRATT & LAMBERT
ORIENTAL NIGHT 29-14

Orchid
GLIDDEN
VESPER 70RB67/067

Pink Rose
GLIDDEN
PEACHGLOW
90YR71/144

Pink Daisy
BENJAMIN MOORE
SMASHING PINK 1303

Water Lily
PRATT & LAMBERT
TULIPE VIOLET 30-14

Magenta Anemone
SHERWIN-WILLIAMS
FORWARD FUSCHIA
SW 6842

Peony
BENJAMIN MOORE
SWEET TAFFY 2086-60

Violet
BENJAMIN MOORE
GENTLE VIOLET
2071-20

Hydrangea
PRATT & LAMBERT
TROOPER 26-14

COLOR INDEX *Shade by Shade*

WHITE

BENJAMIN MOORE
SUPER WHITE INT. RM

**DONALD KAUFMAN
COLOR COLLECTION**
DKC-51

BENJAMIN MOORE
DECORATOR'S WHITE
INT. RM

RALPH LAUREN PAINT
POCKET WATCH WHITE
WW11

FARROW & BALL
ALL WHITE 2005

BENJAMIN MOORE
ACADIA WHITE OC-38

BENJAMIN MOORE
IVORY WHITE 925

**FINE PAINTS
OF EUROPE**
SPINNAKER WHITE 7032

PRATT & LAMBERT
SEED PEARL 27-32

WHITE

BENJAMIN MOORE
SILVER SATIN OC-26

BENJAMIN MOORE
WINTER WHITE 2140-70

**DONALD KAUFMAN
COLOR COLLECTION**
DKC-5

PRATT & LAMBERT
ANTIQUE WHITE 2207

BENJAMIN MOORE
BRILLIANT WHITE

FARROW & BALL
STRONG WHITE 2001

BENJAMIN MOORE
CHINA WHITE INT. RM

FARROW & BALL
POINTING 2003

BENJAMIN MOORE
MAN ON THE MOON
OC-106

COLOR INDEX *Shade by Shade*

CREAM—PALE TAN

BENJAMIN MOORE
LINEN WHITE INT. RM. 70

BENJAMIN MOORE
SWISS COFFEE OC-45

BENJAMIN MOORE
ALABASTER OC-129

BENJAMIN MOORE
POWDER SAND 2151-70

DONALD KAUFMAN COLOR COLLECTION
DKC-28

FARROW & BALL
TALLOW 203

FARROW & BALL
MATCHSTICK 2013

BENJAMIN MOORE
ATRIUM WHITE 79

BENJAMIN MOORE
ATRIUM WHITE INT. RM

TAN—GRAY

**FULL SPECTRUM
PAINTS**
MUSHROOM

BENJAMIN MOORE
QUEEN ANNE PINK HC-60

BENJAMIN MOORE
WHITE CHOCOLATE
OC-127

PRATT & LAMBERT
SILVER LINING 32-32

MODERN MASTERS
PLATINUM ME 591

PRATT & LAMBERT
ARROWROOT 29-32

FARROW & BALL
SLIPPER SATIN 2004

BENJAMIN MOORE
SILKEN PINE 2144-50

PRATT & LAMBERT
PHANTOM 11-31

TAN—GRAY

RALPH LAUREN PAINT
ARCHITECTURAL
CREAM UL 55

**DONALD KAUFMAN
COLOR COLLECTION**
DKC-54

BENJAMIN MOORE
HEAVEN 2118-70

**OLD FASHIONED MILK
PAINT CO.**
OYSTER WHITE

BENJAMIN MOORE
HORIZON 1478

PRATT & LAMBERT
PEARL WHITE 29-29

BENJAMIN MOORE
GRANT BEIGE HC-83

PRATT & LAMBERT
FRESH CREAM 11-5

BENJAMIN MOORE
COASTAL FOG AC-1

TAN—GRAY

FARROW & BALL
BONE 15

BENJAMIN MOORE
BLEEKER BEIGE HC-80

BENJAMIN MOORE
HAMPSHIRE ROCKS 1450

FARROW & BALL
CHARLESTON GRAY 243

BENJAMIN MOORE
SMOKEY TAUPE 983

PRATT & LAMBERT
PELHAM GRAY LIGHT
CW-819

BEIGE

SHERWIN-WILLIAMS
HONIED WHITE 7106

BENJAMIN MOORE
PALE DAFFODIL 2017-60

BENJAMIN MOORE
WINDHAM CREAM HG-6

FARROW & BALL
FARROW'S CREAM 67

FULL SPECTRUM PAINTS
BUTTERCREAM

MYTHIC PAINT
PEBBLE BEACH 167-2

BENJAMIN MOORE
STRAW 2154-50

RALPH LAUREN COLOR COLLECTION
YELLOWHAMMER GH100

SHERWIN-WILLIAMS
IVOIRE SW6127

BEIGE

FARROW & BALL
PALE HOUND 71

SHERWIN-WILLIAMS
HUMBLE GOLD SW6380

PRATT & LAMBERT
AVOINE DE MER 17-26

BENJAMIN MOORE
POWELL BUFF HC-35

FARROW & BALL
DORSET CREAM 68

BENJAMIN MOORE
HEPPLEWHITE IVORY
HC-36

RALPH LAUREN PAINT
CREAM STONE UL54

BENJAMIN MOORE
LAVENDER ICE 2069-60

C2
ENOKI 425

BEIGE

BENJAMIN MOORE
MORNING SUNSHINE
2018-50

**PHILIP'S
PERFECT COLORS**
AGUA VERTE PPC-BL7

**FINE PAINTS
OF EUROPE**
LP-16

SHERWIN-WILLIAMS
PALE EARTH 8133

C2
CHAI 7293

BROWN

FARROW & BALL
STRING 8

SHERWIN-WILLIAMS
WHOLE WHEAT SW6121

BENJAMIN MOORE
PAPAYA 957

BENJAMIN MOORE
SHELBURNE BUFF HC-28

SHERWIN-WILLIAMS
BAGEL 6114

PRATT & LAMBERT
SILVER BLOND 14-29

FARROW & BALL
CLUNCH 2009

C2
CAFÉ LATTE 7314

PRATT & LAMBERT
SOLITARY 19-29

BROWN

BENJAMIN MOORE
CAMEL BACK 1103

FARROW & BALL
SAND 45

FARROW & BALL
BISCUIT 38

BENJAMIN MOORE
VALLEY FORGE BROWN
HC-74

RALPH LAUREN PAINT
CRESTED BUTTE NA40

BENJAMIN MOORE
THICKET AF-405

BENJAMIN MOORE
SEAPEARL OC-19

**DONALD KAUFMAN
COLOR COLLECTION**
DKC-64

C2
QUAHOG 8385

BROWN

**DONALD KAUFMAN
COLOR COLLECTION**
DKC-50

FARROW & BALL
DRAB 41

BENJAMIN MOORE
DANVILLE TAN HC-91

PRATT & LAMBERT
GLOAMING 2145

PRATT & LAMBERT
FLINT 32-20

BENJAMIN MOORE
CARRINGTON BEIGE
HC-93

RALPH LAUREN PAINT
MASTER ROOM VM99

PRATT & LAMBERT
SILVER BIRCH 18-31

BENJAMIN MOORE
WHITALL BROWN HC-69

BROWN

BENJAMIN MOORE
SCARECROW 1041

PHILIP'S PERFECT COLORS
MINK PPC-G13

RALPH LAUREN PAINT
WEATHERED BROWN
UL44

BENJAMIN MOORE
DAVENPORT TAN HC-76

BENJAMIN MOORE
SHENANDOAH TAUPE
AC-36

DUNN-EDWARDS
COCONUT SKIN DE1055

BENJAMIN MOORE
SADDLE SOAP 2110-30

BENJAMIN MOORE
NORTH CREEK
BROWN 1001

BENJAMIN MOORE
DECK ENAMEL RICH
BROWN 60

BROWN

BENJAMIN MOORE
BRANCHPORT BROWN
HC-72

BENJAMIN MOORE
ONYX 2133-10

BENJAMIN MOORE
MUSTANG 2111-30

BENJAMIN MOORE
BROWN SUGAR 2112-20

BENJAMIN MOORE
MOUNTAIN RIDGE 1456

PRATT & LAMBERT
WENDIGO 2293

BENJAMIN MOORE
VAN BUREN BROWN
HC-70

RALPH LAUREN PAINT
DESERT BOOT TH35

BENJAMIN MOORE
CHOCOLATE CANDY
BROWN 2107-10

BROWN

FARROW & BALL
MAHOGANY 36

**DONALD KAUFMAN
COLOR COLLECTION**
DKC-66

VALSPAR
LABRADOR 3009-9

BENJAMIN MOORE
WENGE AF-180

BENJAMIN MOORE
DEEP TAUPE 2111-10

**FINE PAINTS
OF EUROPE**
DUTCH CHOCOLATE 6012

BENJAMIN MOORE
TUDOR BROWN

RALPH LAUREN PAINT
CHOCOLATE SOUFFLÉ
VM90

SHERWIN-WILLIAMS
BRAINSTORM BRONZE
7033

YELLOW

BENJAMIN MOORE
PALE MOON OC-108

BENJAMIN MOORE
GOLDEN STRAW 2152-50

DONALD KAUFMAN
COLOR COLLECTION
DKC-30

C2
CORNBREAD C2-138

BENJAMIN MOORE
GOLDEN HONEY 297

BENJAMIN MOORE
SUNDANCE 2022-50

BENJAMIN MOORE
DALILA 319

RALPH LAUREN PAINT
GOLDFINCH GH105

BENJAMIN MOORE
LITTLE ANGEL 318

YELLOW

BENJAMIN MOORE
SUNBURST 2023-40

**FINE PAINTS
OF EUROPE**
SUNNYSIDE LANE 7014T

BENJAMIN MOORE
SUN-KISSED YELLOW
2022-20

BENJAMIN MOORE
MUSTARD OLIVE 2051-10

PRATT & LAMBERT
CANARY YELLOW 12-8

GLIDDEN
YELLOW GOLD 758

FARROW & BALL
YELLOW GROUND 218

BENJAMIN MOORE
SHOWTIME 923

FARROW & BALL
CITRON 74

YELLOW

FARROW & BALL
BABOUCHE 223

FARROW & BALL
CIARA YELLOW 73

**DONALD KAUFMAN
COLOR COLLECTION**
DKC-20

PRATT & LAMBERT
BEESWAX 11-6

ORANGE

PORTOLA PAINTS
SUMMER SQUASH 022

SHERWIN-WILLIAMS
GUSTO GOLD SW 6904

GLIDDEN
DESERT ORANGE
78YR39/593

ACE PAINT
YUMA B21-6

VALSPAR
SPRING SQUASH 2008-1B

PAPERS AND PAINTS
PERSIAN YELLOW HC15

FARROW & BALL
ORANGERY 70

PRATT & LAMBERT
SUBTLE ORANGE 9-7

BENJAMIN MOORE
CITRUS BLAST 2018-30

ORANGE

BENJAMIN MOORE
ORANGE SKY 2018-10

BENJAMIN MOORE
SOFT PUMPKIN 2166-40

BENJAMIN MOORE
SOFT MARIGOLD 160

BEHR
YAM 290B-7

SHERWIN-WILLIAMS
SUNFLOWER SW 6678

BENJAMIN MOORE
CALYPSO ORANGE
2015-30

RALPH LAUREN PAINT
CALIFORNIA POPPY
GH170

BENJAMIN MOORE
FIRENZE AF-225

**PHILIP'S PERFECT
COLORS**
ADOBE O8

ORANGE

**DONALD KAUFMAN
COLOR COLLECTION**
DKC-35

BENJAMIN MOORE
CORLSBUD CANYON 074

BENJAMIN MOORE
GOLD RUSH 2166-10

SHERWIN-WILLIAMS
DETERMINED ORANGE
6635

BENJAMIN MOORE
AUDUBON RUSSET HC-51

BENJAMIN MOORE
TANGERINE FUSION 083

BENJAMIN MOORE
FRESNO 020

PRATT & LAMBERT
NASTURTIUM 1830

BENJAMIN MOORE
ELECTRIC ORANGE
2015-10

ORANGE

BENJAMIN MOORE
RUMBA ORANGE 2014-20

BENJAMIN MOORE
FESTIVE ORANGE 2014-10

**SYDNEY HARBOUR
PAINT COMPANY**
BLOOD ORANGE

FARROW & BALL
CHARLOTTE'S LOCKS 268

BENJAMIN MOORE
TANGERINE DREAM
2012-30

BENJAMIN MOORE
ORANGE PARROT
2169-20

CALIFORNIA PAINTS
PUMPKIN 16

PRATT & LAMBERT
SPICY 9-16

RALPH LAUREN PAINT
CORK

PINK

BENJAMIN MOORE
LOVE & HAPPINESS 1191

BENJAMIN MOORE
WHEATBERRY 2099-70

BENJAMIN MOORE
OLD COUNTRY OC-76

BENJAMIN MOORE
PALE PINK SATIN 008

RALPH LAUREN PAINT
WALTON CREAM VM65

FARROW & BALL
DIMITY 2008

FARROW & BALL
PINK GROUND 202

VALSPAR
APRICOT ICE 2001-2C

VALSPAR
PARIS PINK MS037

PINK

BENJAMIN MOORE
BLANCHED CORAL 886

SHERWIN-WILLIAMS
WHITE DOGWOOD
SW 6315

BENJAMIN MOORE
SMASHING PINK 1303

PANTONE
705-C

FARROW & BALL
CALAMINE 230

GLIDDEN
PEACHGLOW 90YR71/144

BENJAMIN MOORE
PINK BEGONIA 2078-50

BENJAMIN MOORE
SWEET TAFFY 2086-60

BENJAMIN MOORE
ROMANTIC PINK 2004-70

PINK

GLIDDEN
CHECKERBERRY
32RR50/260

BENJAMIN MOORE
PASSION PINK 2075-60

BENJAMIN MOORE
SPRING LILAC 1388

PORTER PAINTS
PERSIAN PINK 6650-1

GLIDDEN
VESPER 70RB67/067

PORTOLA PAINTS
GERANIUM 005

PITTSBURGH PAINTS
ROSE FANTASY 136-4

BEHR
CANDY COATED 120B-5

SHERWIN-WILLIAMS
IN THE PINK SW 6583

PINK

**FINE PAINTS
OF EUROPE**
COLONIAL ROSE 7102T

BENJAMIN MOORE
CAT'S MEOW 1332

PRATT & LAMBERT
CORAL PINK 2-8

BENJAMIN MOORE
OLD WORLD 2011-40

BENJAMIN MOORE
RED PARROT 1308

BENJAMIN MOORE
CORAL GABLES 2010-40

BENJAMIN MOORE
CORAL PINK 2003-50

FARROW & BALL
FOWLER PINK 39

BENJAMIN MOORE
CORAL REEF 012

HOT PINK

BENJAMIN MOORE
PEONY 2079-30

SHERWIN-WILLIAMS
FORWARD FUSCHIA
SW 6842

BENJAMIN MOORE
PINK CORSAGE 1349

RALPH LAUREN PAINT
RACER PINK 1B07

**SYDNEY HARBOUR
PAINT COMPANY**
PRISCILLA

BENJAMIN MOORE
RAZZLE DAZZLE 1348

BENJAMIN MOORE
DROP DEAD GORGEOUS
1329

BENJAMIN MOORE
MILANO RED 1313

RED

RALPH LAUREN PAINT
CAPRI PINK VM71

BENJAMIN MOORE
CORAL SPICE 2170-40

BENJAMIN MOORE
FLORIDA PINK 1320

FARROW & BALL
MENAGERIE 63

FARROW & BALL
RED EARTH 64

**FINE PAINTS
OF EUROPE**
WINTERSWEET BERRY
5104T

**PAPERS AND
PAINTS LTD.**
MOORISH RED HC55

PORTOLA PAINTS
PAPRIKA 013

BENJAMIN MOORE
WARM SIENNA 1203

RED

FARROW & BALL
BLAZER 212

RALPH LAUREN PAINT
MAITAI IB58

SHERWIN-WILLIAMS
HEARTTHROB SW 6866

RALPH LAUREN PAINT
LIFEVEST ORANGE IB64

BENJAMIN MOORE
RED 2000-10

BENJAMIN MOORE
RUBY RED 2001-10

RALPH LAUREN PAINT
LATTICE RED IB57

**FINE PAINTS
OF EUROPE**
TULIP RED 1001

BENJAMIN MOORE
SALSA 2009-20

RED

BENJAMIN MOORE
REDSTONE 2009-10

PRATT & LAMBERT
VINTAGE CLARET 1013

PRATT & LAMBERT
SCARLET O'HARA 1870

BENJAMIN MOORE
HERITAGE RED EXT. RM.

BENJAMIN MOORE
LADYBUG RED 1322

SHERWIN-WILLIAMS
TANAGER SW 6601

BENJAMIN MOORE
CHILI PEPPER 2004-20

BENJAMIN MOORE
MOROCCAN RED 1309

FARROW & BALL
RECTORY RED 217

RED

BENJAMIN MOORE
MILLION DOLLAR RED
2003-10

BENJAMIN MOORE
MERLOT RED 2006-10

PRATT & LAMBERT
PAGODA RED 5-15

BENJAMIN MOORE
TUCSON RED 1300

RALPH LAUREN PAINT
DRESSAGE RED TH41

RALPH LAUREN PAINT
RELAY RED IB11

BENJAMIN MOORE
SANGRIA 2006-20

**DONALD KAUFMAN
COLOR COLLECTION**
DKC-17

FARROW & BALL
PICTURE GALLERY
RED 42

RED

BENJAMIN MOORE
RUST 2175-30

GLIDDEN
DRUM BEAT 00YR08/409

GREEN

RALPH LAUREN PAINT
BASALT VM121

DUNN-EDWARDS
SOFT MINT DE5686

BENJAMIN MOORE
SWEET DREAMS 847

GREEN

BENJAMIN MOORE
OPAL ESSENCE 680

DONALD KAUFMAN
COLOR COLLECTION
DKC-29

BENJAMIN MOORE
FRESH DEW 435

FARROW & BALL
TERESA'S GREEN 236

BENJAMIN MOORE
WISPY GREEN 414

DURON MOUNT
VERNON ESTATE
OF COLOURS
LEAMON SIRRUP DMV070

DUNN-EDWARDS
RIPE PEAR DE5515

PORTER PAINTS
PARSLEY TINT 6998-1

BENJAMIN MOORE
PALE VISTA 2029-60

COLOR INDEX *Shade by Shade*

GREEN

DUNN-EDWARDS
PERFECT PEAR DE5519

BENJAMIN MOORE
LEMON FREEZE 2025-50

SHERWIN-WILLIAMS
GLEEFUL SW6709

BENJAMIN MOORE
CHIC LIME 396

PRATT & LAMBERT
MOSS GREEN 16-29

DONALD KAUFMAN COLOR COLLECTION
DKC-11

FINE PAINTS OF EUROPE
P11130

PRATT & LAMBERT
SUNNY MEADOW 19-17

BENJAMIN MOORE
POTPOURRI GREEN 2029-50

GREEN

SHERWIN-WILLIAMS
SHAGREEN SW6422

BENJAMIN MOORE
HOLLINGSWORTH GREEN
HC-141

BENJAMIN MOORE
FERNWOOD GREEN
2145-40

**DONALD KAUFMAN
COLOR COLLECTION**
DKC-63

FARROW & BALL
GREEN GROUND 206

**FULL SPECTRUM
PAINTS**
LICHEN

FARROW & BALL
COOKING APPLE
GREEN 32

C2
SALTY BRINE
C2-4388

PRATT & LAMBERT
TAMPICO 1411

GREEN

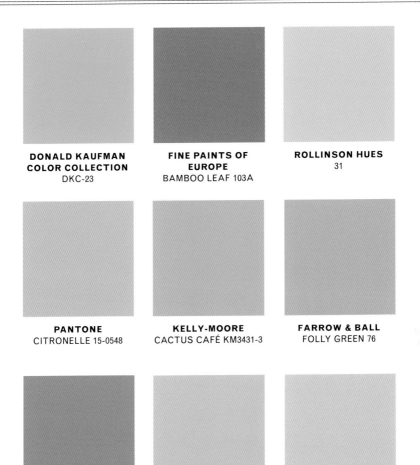

**DONALD KAUFMAN
COLOR COLLECTION**
DKC-23

**FINE PAINTS OF
EUROPE**
BAMBOO LEAF 103A

ROLLINSON HUES
31

PANTONE
CITRONELLE 15-0548

KELLY-MOORE
CACTUS CAFÉ KM3431-3

FARROW & BALL
FOLLY GREEN 76

PANTONE
CRÈME DE MENTHE
16-5919

**FINE PAINTS
OF EUROPE**
2030-G70Y

GLIDDEN
THYME 70YY 46/160

GREEN

FARROW & BALL
BREAKFAST ROOM
GREEN 81

BEHR
OLIVINE 420F-5

BENJAMIN MOORE
CYPRESS GREEN 509

BENJAMIN MOORE
SEA FOAM 2123-60

**OLD FASHIONED
MILK PAINT CO.**
TAVERN GREEN

BENJAMIN MOORE
MADISON AVENUE 759

BENJAMIN MOORE
ARUBA BLUE 2048-30

BENJAMIN MOORE
VENEZUELAN SEA 2054-30

RALPH LAUREN PAINT
OYSTER BAY SS61

GREEN

FARROW & BALL
MERE GREEN 219

SHERWIN-WILLIAMS
LEAPFROG 6431

BENJAMIN MOORE
FOREST MOSS 2146-20

BENJAMIN MOORE
CLEVELAND GREEN 1525

C2
EXPEDITION 162

BENJAMIN MOORE
SEA GLASS PT-330

**DONALD KAUFMAN
COLOR COLLECTION**
DKC-26

BENJAMIN MOORE
PEALE GREEN HC-121

BENJAMIN MOORE
GREAT BARRINGTON
GREEN HC-122

GREEN

BENJAMIN MOORE
OLIVE BRANCH 2143-30

BENJAMIN MOORE
ALLIGATOR ALLEY 441

FARROW & BALL
CARRIAGE GREEN 94

BENJAMIN MOORE
GARDEN CUCUMBER 644

PRATT & LAMBERT
DEEP JUNGLE 21-17

DUNN-EDWARDS
AFTER THE STORM
DE5769

PRATT & LAMBERT
DARK TEAL 21-16

FARROW & BALL
MINSTER GREEN 224

BENJAMIN MOORE
DEEP RIVER 1582

COLOR INDEX *Shade by Shade*

GREEN

PRATT & LAMBERT
BLACKWATCH GREEN
19-17

MARTIN SENOUR
MARKET SQUARE TAVERN
DARK GREEN CW401

BENJAMIN MOORE
ESSEX GREEN EXT. RM

GRAY—GREEN

BENJAMIN MOORE
GOSSAMER BLUE 2123-40

DONALD KAUFMAN
COLOR COLLECTION
DKC-62

DONALD KAUFMAN
COLOR COLLECTION
DKC-10

GRAY—GREEN

BENJAMIN MOORE
SOFT FERN 2144-40

FARROW & BALL
VERT DE TERRE 234

BENJAMIN MOORE
MESQUITE 501

BENJAMIN MOORE
RACCOON HOLLOW 978

FARROW & BALL
SHADED WHITE 201

BEHR
PLANTATION WHITE
WN-18

**DONALD KAUFMAN
COLOR COLLECTION**
DKC-8

FARROW & BALL
HARDWICK WHITE 5

BENJAMIN MOORE
SMOKE EMBERS 1466

GRAY

RALPH LAUREN PAINT
LINEN UL03

BENJAMIN MOORE
STONE HARBOR 2111-50

**BENJAMIN MOORE
COLOR COLLECTION**
ELEPHANT TUSK OC-8

FARROW & BALL
OLD WHITE 4

BENJAMIN MOORE
HORIZON GRAY 2141-50

BENJAMIN MOORE
NANTUCKET GRAY
HC-111

BENJAMIN MOORE
NOVEMBER RAIN 2142-60

SHERWIN-WILLIAMS
MAGNETIC GRAY
SW-7058

FARROW & BALL
LIGHT BLUE 22

BLUE—GRAY

BENJAMIN MOORE
MOUNTAIN MIST 868

GLIDDEN
ANTIQUE SILVER GLN51

PRATT & LAMBERT
ARGENT 1322

BENJAMIN MOORE
COLONY GREEN 694

BENJAMIN MOORE
SPRING MEADOW 486

BENJAMIN MOORE
HEAVENLY BLUE 709

FARROW & BALL
PARMA GRAY 27

FARROW & BALL
GREEN BLUE 84

BENJAMIN MOORE
SAGE TINT 458

BLUE—GREEN

BENJAMIN MOORE
WOODLAWN BLUE
HC-147

BENJAMIN MOORE
PALLADIAN BLUE HC-144

BENJAMIN MOORE
WEDGEWOOD GRAY
HC-146

SHERWIN-WILLIAMS
HAZEL 6471

BENJAMIN MOORE
DOLPHIN'S COVE 722

BENJAMIN MOORE
CEDAR GROVE 444

FARROW & BALL
LICHEN 19

PRATT & LAMBERT
PERIDOT 18-20

BENJAMIN MOORE
BUXTON BLUE HC-149

BLUE—GREEN

PRATT & LAMBERT
COOS BAY 19-31

BENJAMIN MOORE
BLUE SEAFOAM 2056-60

BENJAMIN MOORE
ICEBERG 2122-50

BENJAMIN MOORE
SEA STAR 2123-30

BENJAMIN MOORE
MISTY MEMORIES 2118-60

PRATT & LAMBERT
DELFT BLUE 24-21

RALPH LAUREN PAINT
BLUE-GREEN GH81

DARK GRAY

**OLD FASHIONED
MILK PAINT CO.**
SLATE

BENJAMIN MOORE
GRAYTINT 1611

FARROW & BALL
PIGEON 25

BENJAMIN MOORE
BEAR CREEK 1470

PRATT & LAMBERT
DIPLOMAT GRAY 33-21

GLIDDEN
ICON GREY 1677

FARROW & BALL
DOWN PIPE 26

BENJAMIN MOORE
WOLF GRAY 2127-40

PRATT & LAMBERT
GUNNEL 25-23

DARK GRAY

BENJAMIN MOORE
HOLIDAY WREATH 447

FARROW & BALL
CLAYDON BLUE 87

SHERWIN-WILLIAMS
BLUE HUBBARD 8438

BENJAMIN MOORE
CHEATING HEART 1617

BENJAMIN MOORE
IRON MOUNTAIN 2134-30

BENJAMIN MOORE
DECK ENAMEL BLACK
C-112-80

BLUE

BENJAMIN MOORE
PATRIOTIC WHITE 2135-70

BENJAMIN MOORE
ICY BLUE 2057-70

BENJAMIN MOORE
STONINGTON GRAY
HC-170

BENJAMIN MOORE
WHIRLPOOL 1436

FARROW & BALL
BORROWED LIGHT 235

VALSPAR
WOODLAWN SILVER
BROOK 5001-1B

BENJAMIN MOORE
BLUE ANGEL 2058-70

BENJAMIN MOORE
JAMAICAN AQUA 2048-60

GLIDDEN
CLEAR BLUE SKY GLB15

BLUE

RALPH LAUREN PAINT
PRUSSIAN BLUE VM122

VALSPAR
STILLNESS 7005-2

BENJAMIN MOORE
LOOKOUT POINT 1646

**DONALD KAUFMAN
COLOR COLLECTION**
DKC-96

**DONALD KAUFMAN
COLOR COLLECTION**
DKC-37

**ANN HALL
COLOR DESIGN**
39

BENJAMIN MOORE
GLASS SLIPPER 1632

BENJAMIN MOORE
LAKE PLACID 827

BENJAMIN MOORE
SUMMER SHOWER 2135-60

BLUE

BENJAMIN MOORE
BIRD'S EGG 2051-60

BENJAMIN MOORE
MORNING GLORY 785

RALPH LAUREN PAINT
MYSTIC RIVER SS21

FARROW & BALL
BLUE GROUND 210

SHERWIN-WILLIAMS
VERDITER BLUE
DCR078 NRH

BENJAMIN MOORE
FLORIDA KEYS BLUE
2050-40

BENJAMIN MOORE
COOL AQUA 2056-40

PARKER PAINT
BLUE TOILE 748

PARKER PAINT
WATERSIDE 7573M

BLUE

BENJAMIN MOORE
RHYTHM AND BLUES 758

VASPAR
EXOTIC SEA 5004-10B

BENJAMIN MOORE
OCEAN BREEZE 2058-60

BENJAMIN MOORE
CAYMAN BLUE 2060-50

BENJAMIN MOORE
BLUE WAVE 2065 -50

BENJAMIN MOORE
JAMESTOWN BLUE
HC-148

BENJAMIN MOORE
NORTHERN AIR 1676

FARROW & BALL
CHINESE BLUE 90

BENJAMIN MOORE
BLUE BELLE 782

BLUE

VALSPAR
LYNDHURST CELESTIAL
BLUE 5003-9C

BENJAMIN MOORE
SAILOR'S SEA BLUE
2063-40

BENJAMIN MOORE
UTAH SKY 2065-40

BENJAMIN MOORE
CLEAREST OCEAN BLUE
2064-40

MODERN MASTERS
VENETIAN BLUE ME-429

PRATT & LAMBERT
LAMBERT'S BLUE
25-13

BENJAMIN MOORE
PADDINGTON BLUE
791

RALPH LAUREN PAINT
BALTIC BLUE IB86

PRATT & LAMBERT
WINDSOR BLUE 27-19

BLUE

BENJAMIN MOORE
DARK TEAL 2053-20

BENJAMIN MOORE
SANTA MONICA BLUE 776

PORTOLA PAINTS
BLUE CART 094

C2
ELECTRIC 275

**FINE PAINTS
OF EUROPE**
DELFT BLUE 4003

BENJAMIN MOORE
CALIFORNIA BLUE
2060-20

BENJAMIN MOORE
VAN DEUSEN BLUE
HC-156

BENJAMIN MOORE
STUNNING 826

BENJAMIN MOORE
DARK ROYAL BLUE
2065-20

BLUE

SHERWIN-WILLIAMS
MORNING GLORY
SW 6971

PRATT & LAMBERT
BLUEBERRY MYRTILLE
1208-3

BENJAMIN MOORE
DOWN POUR BLUE
2063-20

C2
SORCERER 5326

BENJAMIN MOORE
NEWBURYPORT BLUE
HC-155

BENJAMIN MOORE
STARRY NIGHT BLUE
2067-20

FARROW & BALL
HAGUE BLUE 30

BENJAMIN MOORE
MIDNIGHT NAVY 2067-10

BENJAMIN MOORE
CARBON COPY 2117-10

PURPLE

BENJAMIN MOORE
LAVENDER SECRET 1415

BENJAMIN MOORE
MISTY LILAC 2071-70

BENJAMIN MOORE
SPRING IRIS 1402

SHERWIN-WILLIAMS
STUDIO MAUVE 0062

GLIDDEN
LIMOGES BLUE 30BG56/045

BEHR'S DISNEY HOME
CLASSIC POOH
BUTTERFLY FLUTTER BY
DC2A-10-1

BENJAMIN MOORE
PEACE AND HAPPINESS
1380

C2
BELLA DONNA C2-316W

BENJAMIN MOORE
WINDMILL WINGS 2067-60

PURPLE

SHERWIN-WILLIAMS
SASSY BLUE 1241

BENJAMIN MOORE
JET STREAM 814

BENJAMIN MOORE
FRENCH LILAC 1403

BENJAMIN MOORE
ORIENTAL IRIS 1418

BENJAMIN MOORE
RIVIERA AZURE 822

PRATT & LAMBERT
AUTUMN CROCUS 1141

BENJAMIN MOORE
PERSIAN VIOLET 1419

BENJAMIN MOORE
SUMMER BLUE 2067-50

BENJAMIN MOORE
BRAZILIAN BLUE 817

PURPLE

PRATT & LAMBERT
TROOPER 26-14

RALPH LAUREN PAINT
CALYPSO VM138

PRATT & LAMBERT
TULIPE VIOLET 30-14

PRATT & LAMBERT
ROSA LEE 1-13

DUNN-EDWARDS
DEEP CARNATION DE5011

PRATT & LAMBERT
ORIENTAL NIGHT 29-14

BENJAMIN MOORE
GENTLE VIOLET 2071-20

PRATT & LAMBERT
JACK HORNER'S PLUM
1-20

BENJAMIN MOORE
MYSTICAL GRAPE 2071-30

PURPLE

BENJAMIN MOORE
PASSION PLUM 2073-30

BENJAMIN MOORE
BLACK RASPBERRY
2072-20

BENJAMIN MOORE
GRAPPA 1393

C2
WICKED 6446

BENJAMIN MOORE
CAPONATA AF-650

DESIGNER INDEX

Michael Smith
  Coos Bay 19-31 by PL, 101
  Silver Blond 14-29 by PL, 42
Windsor Smith
  Pink Begonia 2078-50 by BM, 159
  Ripe Pear DE5515 by DE, 174
Matthew Patrick Smyth
  Beeswax 11-6 by PL, 214
  Linen White 70 by BM, 40
  Vintage Claret 1013 by PL, 140
  Wickham Gray HC-171 by BM, 57
William Sofield
  Persian Yellow HC 15 by PP, 147
Ruthie Sommers
  Blue Seafoam 2056-60 by BM, 62
  Iceberg 2122-50 by BM, 54
  Sea Foam 2123-60 by BM, 246
Rebecca Tier Soskin
  Apricot Ice 2001-2C by VS, 264
Alison Spear
  Ruby Red 2001-10 by BM, 153
Whitney Stewart
  Café Latte 7314 by C2, 209
  Caponata AF-650 by BM, 199
  Chai 7293 by C2, 209
  Electric 275 by C2, 60
  Enoki 425 by C2, 225
  Gold Rush 2166-10 by BM, 218
  Olive Branch 2143-30 by BM, 218
  Quahog 8385 by C2, 80
  Thicket AF-405 by BM, 199
Robert Stilin
  Cooking Apple Green 32 by FB, 136
Stephanie Stokes
  Claydon Blue 87 by FB, 188
  Fresh Dew 435 by BM, 107
Sara Story
  Calamine 230 by FB, 129
  Dark Teal 21-16 by PL, 144
Tom Stringe
  Prussian Blue VM122 by RLP, 208
Madeline Stuart
  Light Blue 22 by FB, 17
  Pale Hound 71 by FB, 49
Rob Stuart
  Antique Silver GLN51 by GL, 149

James Swan
  Pearl White 29-29 by PL, 270
  POR2343 FB by PL, 271
  Rosa Lee 1-13 by PL, 270

Rose Tarlow
  All White 2005 by FB, 24
  Pointing 2003 by FB, 24
  Slipper Satin 2004 by FB, 24
Jackie Terrell
  Gloaming 2145 by PL, 257
  Lemon Freeze 2025-50 by BM, 248
  Nasturtium 1830 by PL, 257
  Paris Pink MS037 by VS, 160
Suzanne Tucker
  Thyme 70YY 46/160 by GL, 171
  Tulip Red 1001 by FPE, 216

Priscilla Ulmann
  Yellow Ground 218 by FB, 107

Erinn Valencich
  Deep Carnation DE5011 by DE, 227
  Labrador 3009-9 by VS, 261
  Yuma B21-6 by Ace Paint, 185
Peter Vaughn
  Mauve Bauhaus 1407 by BM, 141
  Spring Iris 1402 by BM, 141
Diana Vreeland
  Red 2000-10 by BM, 154, 155

Basil Walter
  DKC-50 by DKC, 200
  DKC-63 by DKC, 200
Marshall Watson
  DKC-37 by DKC, 122
  Humble Gold SW6380 by SW, 188
Kelly Wearstler
  Coral Pink 2-8 by PL, 160
  Delft Blue 24-21 by PL, 52
  Scarlet O'Hara 1870 by PL, 210
  Seed Pearl 27-32 by PL, 37
  Sunny Meadow 19-17 by PL, 174
Barbara Westbrook
  DKC-5 by DKC, 26
  Overcast OC-43 by BM, 193
  Whitall Brown HC-69 by BM, 193

Michael Whaley
  Cedar Grove 444 by BM, 270
  Garden Cucumber 644 by BM, 191
  Lavender Secret 1415 by BM, 131
Timothy Whealon
  Basalt VM121 by RLP, 248
  Northern Air 1676 by BM, 126
Matthew White
  Spring Meadow 486 by BM, 40
Jeannette Whitson
  Hague Blue 30 by FB, 264
Ashley Whittaker
  Mountain Mist 868 by BM, 130
  Peale Green HC-121 by BM, 177
Kendall Wilkinson
  Jet Stream 814 by BM, 273
  Linen White 70 by BM, 273
  39 by Ann Hall Color Design, 67
Bunny Williams
  Cleveland Green 1525 by BM, 169
Bret Witke
  Powder Sand 2151-70 by BM, 115
Ann Wolf
  Firenze AF-225 by BM, 185
Vicente Wolf
  Graytint 1611 by BM, 50
  Patriotic White 2135-70 by BM, 28
Honey Wolters
  November Rain 2142-60 by BM, 54
Eldon Wong
  Classic Pooh Butterfly Flutter By DC2A-10-1 by BR Disney Home, 80
  Redstone 2009-10 by BM, 152
Ron Woodson
  Leapfrog 6341 by SW, 91

Jack Young
  Coral Spice 2170-40 by BM, 48
John Yunis
  Sunnyside Lane 7014T by FPE, 136

INDEX

PHOTO CREDITS

Lucas Allen: 167
Mali Azima: 161
Christopher Baker: 61, 84, 114
Gordon Beall: 20, 244
John Bessler: 44, 53, 168
Brantley Photography: 74
Afshin Chamasmany: 66
Alexander Chernyakov/iStock: 145
Courtesy of Courtney Coleman: 181
Jonn Coolidge: 87
Billy Cunningham: 146
Roger Davies: 17, 49, 228
Carlos Domenech: 164
Courtesy of Clare Donohue: 94
Pieter Estersohn: 5, 26, 128, 152, 193
Richard Felber: 121
Don Freeman: 2, 14, 30, 36, 46, 54, 63, 104, 106, 134, 211, 233, 243, 247, 255, 258
J. Savage Gibson: 19, 25, 51
Oberto Gili: 33, 190
Tria Giovan: 78, 118, 123, 156
Sam Gray: 271
Gridley + Graves: 76
Tom Grimes: 69
Michael Grimm: 81

Bret Gum: 124
Ken Gutmaker: 216
Mick Hales: 202
John M. Hall: 148
Ken Hayden: 230
Alec Hemer: 127
Anice Hoachlander/HD Photo: 226
Horst P. Horst/Condé Nast: 155
Nick Johnson: 162
Courtesy of Ellen Kennon / www. ellenkennon.com: 170
Timothy Kolk: 225, 240, 268
Francesco Lagnese: 201
Eric Laignel: 142
Thomas Loof: 183, 263
Peter Margonelli: 38
Ellen McDermott: 97, 108, 235, 274–275, 276–277
Norman McGrath: 220
Jeff McNamara: 56
James Merrell: 130, 173
Karyn Millet: 41, 91, 92, 223
Matthew Millman: 206
Laura Moss: 65
Ngoc Minh Ngo: 86, 98, 139, 150, 186, 189
Brendan Paul: 29, 209
Victoria Pearson: 72, 158, 212

Eric Piasecki: 88, 111, 176
Eric Piasecki/OTTO: 175
José Picayo: 58
Terry Pommett: 215
Michael Price: 82
Lisa Romerein: 42, 100
Lauren Rubinstein: 256
Patrik Rytikangas: 194
Nathan Schroder: 35
Courtesy of Annie Selke Companies: 219
Tim Street-Porter: 89, 113, 178, 238, 250, 252, 273
Simon Upton: 116, 196
Jonny Valiant: 184
Melissa Valladares: 260
Courtesy of Peter Vaughn: 141
Peter Vitale: 22
Dominique Vorillon: 90
William Waldron: 137, 204
Julian Wass: 71
Simon Watson: 264, 267
Corey Weiner: 249
Ricky Zehavi: 102